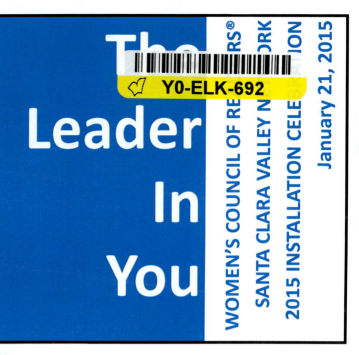

The

Leader

In

You

WOMEN'S COUNCIL OF REALTORS®
SANTA CLARA VALLEY NETWORK
2015 INSTALLATION CELEBRATION
January 21, 2015

Y0-ELK-692

Santa Clara Valley Network

Women's Council of REALTORS ®
Mission Statement

We are a network of successful REALTORS®,
advancing women as professionals and leaders
in business, the industry and the communities we serve.

A Message From Mimi

*I*t's been a busy and amazing 2014 as President of the Santa Clara Valley Chapter of the Women's Council of Realtors. It hasn't been without its challenges throughout the year, promoting and building the organization, mentoring new members, and attending leadership training. I would have never had become the person I am today without this organization – The Woman's Council of Realtors. It has been a great experience for me, and I could have never have done it without my team helping me along the way, like Sheryl Martinez, Matt Nguyen, Thora Tam, Laura Welch, and others.

Looking ahead, I welcome 2015. Our new focus for the year will be developing "The Leader In You." I met many great women leaders in the real estate industry from the Women's Council of Realtors, NAR, CAR, SILVAR, SCCAOR and other associations throughout the nation. They were outstanding role models for me to follow, and I cherish those great relationships. My goal as the 2015 president is to help other individuals grow in our industry, so that they too can become the great leaders found throughout the WCR organization. If you want to build a network with other successful professionals, ranging from the local, state, or national levels, the Women's Council of Realtors is the way to accomplish that. The Women's Council of Realtors is here to help turn your potential as a leader into actual leadership ability.

Are you ready to be a successful leader? Our team is here to help you.

Women's Council of Realtors
Santa Clara Valley Chapter
2014 Leadership Team

PRESIDENT
Mimi Wang, REALTOR®,
GRI, SRES, CDPE, HAFA, REO, CCRM
Century 21 M&M and Associates
(408) 569-3808, mimi@mimihomes.com

PRESIDENT ELECT
Beatriz Supnet, REALTOR®
Fireside Realty
(408) 568-6959, beatriz550@aol.com

TREASURER/SECRETARY
Sonia Walia, Sr. Mortgage Loan Originator
Stearns Lending
(415) 933-7472 , swalia@stearns.com

MEMEMBERSHIP DIRECTOR
Claudine Rydquist, REALTOR®
Intero Real Estate
(650) 210-6117, crydquist@interorealestate.com

PROGRAM DIRECTOR
Sheryl Martinez, REALTOR®
Aalis Platinum Properties
(408) 209-7674, Sheryl@sherylmartinez.com

VP MARKETING
Matt Nguyen, Loan Officer
US Bank
(408) 784-1846, matt.nguyen@usbank.com

NETWORKING DIRECTOR
Thora Tam, Interior Decorator
Decorating Den Interiors
(408) 223-7300, thoratam@decoratingden.com

Installation Luncheon Program

Welcome – Masters of Ceremonies:
Matt Nguyen, 2014 Membership Director
Thora Tam, 2014 Treasurer/Secretary
Pledge of Allegiance

Inspiration

Introduction of Special Guests

Special Acknowledgements - Mimi Wang

*Keynote Message -*Jason Buzi

Installation of 2015 Officers

Linda Lee, 2015 California State President

Celebratory Toast

Remarks – Mimi Wang

Raffle Prize Drawing

Strategic Partners

Bank of America
Home Loans

Christine Collier
Bank of America
Home Loans Manager
2880 Stevens Creek Blvd.
NMLS ID: 633057
(408) 615-6079
http://mortgage.bankofamerica.com/christinejpugelli
christina.j.pugelli@bankofamerica.com

Strategic Partners

Stearns®

Sonia Walia, MBA
Sterns
Senior Mortgage Loan Originator
39420 Liberty Street, Suite 155
Fremont, CA. 94539
NMLS ID: 1854
(408) 933-7472
www.soniawalia.com
swalia@stearns.com

MLNARIK
THE MLNARIK LAW GROUP, INC.

John Mlnarik
The Mlnarik Law Group
2930 Bowers Avenue
Santa Clara, CA 95051
www.mlnariklaw.com
(408) 919-0088
john@mlnariklaw.com
barry@mlnariklaw.com

Upcoming Events
and Programs in 2015

(Subject to change)

January 21 – Installation Celebration

January 26-27– State Meetings in Palm Desert

March - TBA - Members Only Event*

April 8 - Leadership Forum*

April 20-21 – State Meetings in Sacramento

May - Special Event**—TBA

May 14-16 – National Meetings in DC

June 3 - Technology*

August - TBA - Special Event** - FASHION SHOW

August 7-9 – Leadership Academy in Chicago (By Invitation Only)

September 2 – Chapter Elections and Civic Environment*

October 4-5 – State meetings in San Jose

November 4 - Business Planning and Development for 2016*

November 11-15 – National Meetings in San Diego

November - Members Only Event*

December – TBA - Installation Celebration

Network Leadership Meetings will be held quarterly, for more information, contact Mimi Wang, REALTOR®: 408-569-3808 mimi@mimihomes.com

For information regarding membership, contact Claudine Rydquist, REALTOR®: 650-210-6117 crydquist@interorealestate.com

*For information regarding programs, contact Sheryl Martinez, REALTOR®: 408-209-7674 Sheryl@sherylmartinez.com

**For Information regarding special events, contact Matt Nguyen of Special Events Director: 408-784-1846 matt.nguyen@usbank.com

Past Presidents

2014 Mimi Wang
2013 Melanie Holthaus
2012 Anna Maria Valenzuela
2011 Sheryl Martinez
2010 Amy Ericksen
2009 Pauline Martinez
2008 Patricia Hairston
2007 Katie Kane
2006 Janice Levin
2005 Barbara Lymberis
2004 Dawn O'Neal
2003 Nancy Domich
2002 Jan Miners
2001 Tish Shaikh
2000 Nannette Johnston
1999 Charlene Oxoby
1998 Sherry Wilson
1997 Rose Huggins
1996 Carol de Losada
1995 Naomi Blais
1994 Michi Olson
1993 Karlene Westfall
1992 Nancy Cuddy
1991 Gloria Estes
1990 Pamela Foley
1989 Betty Bennett
1988 Mary Martin
1987 Patricia Engels
1986 Ellen Longworth
1985 Ellen Pinto
1984 Joan Valor
1983 Alexandra McDonald
1982 Shirlee Thompson
1981 Mary Ann Young
1980 D. JoAnn Barr
1979 Norma McDonald

1978 Carole Lushbaugh
1977 Connie Kreps
1976 Catherine Aymar
1975 Peggy Trisler
1974 Glenna Thomas
1973 Evelyn Davis
1972 Helen Moran
1971 Aurora Berryman
1970 Beverly Peterson
1969 Tanya Bryant
1968 Marie Rose Gaspar
1967 Mary Morris
1966 Helen Memullen
1965 Juanita McLaren
1964 Alyce Sunseri
1963 Anne Rosekind
1962 Marie Clare Lopez
1961 Louise Hestwood
1960 Claudia Kratz
1959 Marie Rose Gaspar
1958 Ruth Lederman
1957 Louise Nicols
1956 Vernie Eppie
1955 Connie Russo
1954 F.M. Johnson
1953 Wilma Brown
1952 Henrietta Cauhare

Strategic Partners

Welcome One Of Our Newest Strategic Partners

GRAEBEL® Peace of Mind. Worldwide.^{SM}

Thomas Silvius
Moving Consultant
Graebel Moving Services
2020 S. 10th St, SJ 95112
(408) 425-0947
tsilvius@graebel.com

Scott Gordon

THE NEW
REVERSE MORTGAGE

ISBN: 978-0-9889619-3-7 Paperback
ISBN: 978-0-9889619-5-1 eBook
ISBN: 978-0-9889619-4-4 Kindle

Cover art by Jeff Brosch
Book layout and e-book design by Velin@Perseus-Design.com

For information, contact:

Scott A. Gordon, Open Mortgage, LLC
14101 W Hwy 290 #1300
Austin, TX 78737
T: 512-492-3306
ScottGordon@openmtg.com
OpenMortgage.com
JoinOpenMortgage.com

To my wife, Tana, for supporting me in all I do.

I would also like to acknowledge the support and efforts of so many people who have helped me with this book. My senior staff, Richard Woodruff, Greg Block, Joe Morris, Diane Creasy, Brian McKinney, Laura Kardow, and Jim Howard make it possible for me to have time to work on a book.

Special thanks to Joe Morris in the Reverse Division, and Wayne Conley, Dan Scerpella, Phil Risch, Sara Deere, Charles Guinn, and Rick Sweeney for their help reviewing and correcting chapters. They are all great originators and their experience helped a lot.

Thanks to Susan Seawolf Hayes for her help editing and improving the book, and to Velin Saramov who always does a great job on layout and more.

Table of Contents

How to Read This Book

This book contains lots of information about reverse mortgages, including a little history, a definition section, and the requirements to qualify. If you are a little dyslexic (as I am), don't have time for the whole book or only care about one or two topics, feel free to skip right to the relevant chapters.

Chapter 1 covers the history of reverse mortgage, a topic you may find interesting but one which doesn't really reflect the nature of current programs and how they can help you today. It's fine to skip this chapter.

Chapter 2-4 speak to today's reverse mortgage, addressing the myths surrounding them and true stories of "reverses," as they're often called. I believe all readers should read these chapters!

Chapter 5 deals with speaking to your adult children or your senior parents about finances and a possible reverse mortgage. You may find it helpful, or you might not need it.

Chapters 6-9 are the real meat of the book. If you skip everything else, you should read Chapters 6-9 to learn if you are eligible, how you qualify, how you go through the process, and how to pay off the loan.

Chapter 10 is a very interesting topic, HECM [home equity conversion mortgage] for purchase, or how to purchase more home with a reverse mortgage and have no payment. Great if you are purchasing your retirement home!

Chapter 11 offers fresh financial strategies for using a reverse mortgage, aside from the original scenario of seniors in financial need using a reverse mortgage to access home equity. This chapter teaches you how to stretch your retirement dollars, protect other assets or accomplish other goals while you're still kicking.

Appendices 1-3 contain information about retirement expenses, helpful government benefits and other financial planning topics.

Appendix 4 contains information on saving for retirement.

Introduction

A reverse mortgage is a special type of home loan that allows the homeowner to stop making house payments and possibly convert some of the equity in their home into cash. While reverse mortgages originally arose to act as emergency solutions, now seniors are using them as an added financial tool to stretch retirement finances. There are many possible benefits to a reverse mortgage, including:

- **Financial flexibility** - Seniors have greater financial flexibility with a reverse mortgage. A reverse mortgage can stretch other savings much further.

- **Ability to meet financial obligations** – Whether faced with a mountain of medical expenses or just a desire to become debt free, seniors can use a reverse mortgage to meet (and exceed) their financial obligations.

- **Making needed home improvements** – Some seniors find it difficult to keep up with necessary home maintenance.

Whether to replace a leaky roof or the air conditioning and heating system, a reverse mortgage can provide funds for such repairs.

- **Less stressful life** – Too many seniors live with stress and worry because of their financial situation. Stress takes a toll on both mental and physical health, and a reverse mortgage can help seniors greatly reduce the stress in their lives.

- **Having extra money to travel** – Many seniors would like to travel and see the world, or just visit family and friends. A reverse mortgage can help make these dreams come true.

As you can see, a reverse mortgage offers many exciting benefits, which is why more Americans are exploring this intriguing options.

For background information:

Planning for retirement, see Appendix A1.

Government safety nets, see Appendix A2.

Saving for Retirement, see Appendix A3.

1.

History and Original Intent of Reverse Mortgages

Since the 1970s, parties have sought to create mortgage instruments that would enable senior homeowners obtain loans to convert equity into income, while providing that no repayments would be due for a specified period or, ideally, for the lifetime of the borrower. These instruments have come to be known as "reverse mortgages," "reverse annuity mortgages" or "home equity conversion loans."

Reverse mortgages are the opposite of traditional mortgages in the sense that the borrower receives payments from the lender instead of making payments to the lender. Reverse mortgages enable senior homeowners to remain in their homes while using their home equity as a form of income.

In general, reverse mortgage distributions may take one of four forms: term, tenure, line of credit, or lump sum. Under a term option, the borrower receives income for a specified period. Depending on how much the borrower elects to receive, the available cash could conceivably run out. Under the tenure option, the borrower receives income for as long as he continues to occupy the property.

The next option is the line of credit. In this scenario the borrower can access cash when he needs it, as opposed to having automatic distributions. Some borrowers actually set the line of credit up strictly as a rainy day or special occasion fund. The final distribution option is the lump sum. The borrowers might take all the money available as cash at closing (currently they can take 60% at closing and the remaining 40% in one year); or, in the case of some loans, take 60% at closing in a fixed rate scenario and no more after that. With lump sum distributions, interest accrues on the loan balance more quickly. This is also true when a borrower is refinancing an existing mortgage and a large amount of cash is distributed to pay off the previous lender, with remaining amounts, if any, to be taken in any of the four options. Offsetting the faster interest accrual is the fact that this results in immediate positive gains to the borrower's monthly cash flow since he no longer must make monthly mortgage principal and interest payments. Taxes and Insurance remain the responsibility of the reverse mortgage borrower, however.

For borrowers, the most risky reverse mortgage option is the term distribution. Borrowers have been reluctant to select this option because at the end of the loan term, the borrower receives no more distributions from the loan. This might cause the borrower to have to sell the home.

For lenders, the most risky reverse mortgage option is the tenure distribution option. Lenders have been reluctant to originate such mortgages because the borrower is guaranteed lifetime income and lifetime occupancy of the home, a risky scenario because the mortgage debt grows over time, and the debt could exceed the value of the home if the borrower lives longer than his or her life expectancy.

The use of tenure reverse mortgages has grown in recent years due to the availability of a Federal Housing Administration (FHA)-insured reverse mortgage. With an FHA-backed tenure reverse mortgage, the risk of the borrower living too long shifts to the federal government.

Under prior law, an FHA mortgage limit based on the location of the property applied to all FHA-insured reverse mortgages. However, the Housing and Economic Recovery Act of 2008, P.L. 110-289, established a mortgage limit equal to the conforming loan limit for the Federal Home Loan Mortgage Corporation (Freddie Mac). (The conforming loan limit is the maximum loan amount Fannie Mae or Freddie Mac will purchase.)

According to the U.S. Dept. of Housing and Urban Development (HUD) American Housing Survey (AHS) (December, 2013), there are about 18.3 million senior homeowners (age 65 or older), and the median value of their homes is $168,654.

About 12.5 million, or more than 68% of senior homeowners have no mortgage debt. In fact, equity in their homes represents the largest asset for many senior homeowners. But senior homeowners find that although inflation has increased the value of their homes, it has also eroded the purchasing power of their fixed incomes. They find it increasingly difficult to maintain their homes while also paying for needed food, medical, and other expenses.

Because of low income, many may be unable to qualify for loans for unexpected expenses. "House rich and cash poor" is the phrase often used to describe this dilemma. One option is to sell the home and move to rental housing or purchase a lower-cost home. For a variety of reasons, however, many older Americans prefer to remain in the homes in which they may have spent most of their working years.

Since the 1970s, academics and housing advocates have sought to create mortgage instruments that would enable senior homeowners to obtain loans to convert their equity into income, while providing that no repayments would be due for a specified period or, ideally, for the lifetime of the borrower.

These instruments have been referred to as reverse mortgages, reverse annuity mortgages, and home equity conversion loans. Generally, when a borrower obtains a mortgage, a lender advances a lump-sum payment to or on behalf of the borrower, and the borrower becomes committed to making a stream of monthly payments to repay the loan. With the reverse mortgage, the lender becomes committed to making a stream of payments to the borrower, and such payments are repaid to the lender in a lump sum at some future date.

Thus, reverse mortgages are the opposite of traditional mortgages in that the borrower receives payments from the lender instead of making such payments to the lender. Reverse mortgages are designed to enable senior homeowners to remain in their homes while using the equity in their homes as a form of income.

Although reverse mortgages are a small part of the total mortgage market, their use has increased substantially in recent years.

Evolution of Reverse Mortgages

Early Days

The very first reverse mortgage originated in Portland, Maine in 1961, but it wasn't until 1977 that the first statewide deferred payment loan originated in Wisconsin. Then in 1980 the "Home Equity Conversion Project" was funded by the U.S. Dept. of Health and Human Services Administration on Aging.

Sale-Leaseback Transactions

Early predecessors of reverse mortgages were known as sale-leaseback transactions. Under a sale-leaseback transaction, the buyer buys a property and simultaneously leases it to a seller. Often businesses seeking to raise working capital utilized sale-leaseback transactions to sell and lease back property used in the trade or business, a technique enabling firms to raise capital and avoid high borrowing costs. Thus capital formerly frozen in real estate assets became free to generate a higher rate of return in the business itself. If the business obtained a mortgage against that property, normally the mortgage would cover only 75 to 80% of the market value of the property. However, through a sale-leaseback transaction, the business could obtain cash for 100% of the property value (less transaction costs) and still maintain use and possession of the property.

In the 1970s, housing advocates began to suggest sale-leaseback transactions as a way for senior homeowners to convert equity in their homes into a source of income. Under this plan, the senior homeowner would sell the home and lease it back from the new owner. The seller could retain the right of occupancy for life or for a fixed number of years. In either case, the seller would become a renter of the home that he or she formerly owned.

The triple burden of home maintenance, taxes and insurance could make it difficult for some seniors to remain in their homes, causing them to make trade-offs between home-related expenses and necessities such as food and health care. Such trade-offs might result in owner-occupied but substandard property. Under a sale-leaseback plan, the owner/investor would pay operating costs of the property and gain associated tax write-offs.

Proponents of the sale-leaseback plan note that the senior could remain in a well maintained home without the financial burden of such maintenance. But the sale-leaseback plan is a complicated form of equity conversion because of the number of variables that must be negotiated between the buyer and seller, including sales price, down payment, loan term and lease agreement. In addition, these items are interrelated and may affect the net benefit of the transaction to the senior homeowner.

A few of these sale-leaseback programs sprang up; for instance, under the so-called "Grannie Mae" program, a company would arrange for the children or grandchildren to purchase and leaseback the home of a senior. Under another plan, the Fouratt Senior Citizen

Equity Plan, the leaseback payments took two forms: a promissory note (mortgage) and a deferred annuity. The promissory note provided for monthly payments to the seller over a term equal to the greater of the seller's life expectancy or 10 years. When the payments from the promissory note ended, the annuity would make the same payments for the lifetime of the seller. But only three Grannie Mae loans were made; and although there was interest in the Fouratt program, no loans were ever made. However, even today some senior housing advocates favor sale-leaseback transactions as an option for senior homeowners.

Recent Reverse Mortgage Plans

Over time three major reverse mortgage products became available to consumers in the U.S: the Home Equity Conversion Mortgage Program (HECM), the Home Keeper reverse mortgage, and the Cash Account Plan. (At present, a relatively new reverse mortgage, the "Senior Equity Reverse Mortgage," is only available in Arizona, California, Delaware, the District of Columbia, Florida, Georgia, Maryland, North Carolina, South Carolina, Texas, and Virginia.

All of the plans provide the borrower with lifetime occupancy of the home—"tenure" reverse mortgages. It is this availability of tenure reverse mortgages that is like behind the dramatic growth of reverse mortgages in the past few years. These tenure reverse mortgages also provide the borrower with flexibility on how the homeowner received the income. A borrower may receive monthly payments as long as the she occupies the property. The borrower may receive a line of credit which grows at a specified annual rate and from which the borrower may make draws as needed. The borrower may choose to receive a large up-front cash advance, or the borrower may choose any combination of the above, such as a smaller cash advance, a line of credit and/or monthly income.

Home Equity Conversion Mortgage Program (HECM)

The Housing and Community Development Act of 1987 authorized the Home Equity Conversion Mortgage Program (HECM) through the Department of Housing and Urban Development (HUD) as a demonstration program. It was the first nationwide reverse mortgage program which offered the possibility of lifetime occupancy to senior homeowners. As noted above, such mortgages are referred to as tenure reverse mortgages. The borrowers must be senior homeowners who own and occupy their homes. The interest rate on the loan may be fixed or adjustable.

The homeowner and the lender may agree to share in any future appreciation in the value of the property.

The program is now considered permanent, with the law amended to permit its use for residences containing one to four units if the owner occupies one of the units.

The borrower may choose from five payment plans:

- *Tenure* - equal monthly payments as long as at least one borrower lives in and continues to occupy the property as a principal residence.

- *Term* - equal monthly payments for a fixed period of months selected by the borrower.

- *Line of Credit* - installments at times and in an amount of the borrower's choosing until the line of credit is exhausted.

- *Modified Tenure* - combination of line of credit with monthly payments for as long as the borrower remains in the home.

- *Modified Term* - combination of line of credit with monthly payments for a fixed period of months selected by the borrower.

Prior law provided that the HECM loan may not exceed the Federal Housing Administration (FHA) mortgage limit for the property area. The Housing and Economic Recovery Act of 2008 establishes a national HECM limit equal to the conforming loan limit for the Federal Home Loan Mortgage Corporation (Freddie Mac).

The mortgage must be a first mortgage, which in essence implies that any previous mortgage must be fully repaid either prior to the HECM or from the initial proceeds of the HECM.

Prior to obtaining a loan, borrowers must receive appropriate counseling by third parties who will explain the financial implications of entering into home equity conversion mortgages as well as explain the options, other than home equity conversion mortgages, that may be available to senior homeowners.

To prevent displacement of the senior homeowners, HECMs must include terms that give the homeowner the option of deferring repayment of the loan until the death of the homeowner, the voluntary sale of the home, or the occurrence of some other event as prescribed by HUD regulations. The borrowers may prepay the loans without penalty.

Borrowers are required to purchase insurance from FHA. The insurance serves three purposes:

(1) Protection for lenders from suffering losses if the final loan balance exceeds the proceeds from the sale of a home,

(2) Continuance of monthly payments to the homeowner if the lender defaults on the loan and

(3) Protection for borrowers and/or their inheritors if the loan balance exceeds the value of the home at the time of repayment. Among other things, the insurance provides that other assets of a borrower's estate or his inheritors cannot be used to repay the reverse mortgage. The loan is collateralized solely by the home.

At loan origination, borrowers must pay an up-front mortgage insurance premium (MIP) of 1/2% of the maximum mortgage amount. In addition, borrowers pay an annual insurance premium of 0.5% of the loan balance. Borrowers do not directly pay the insurance premiums. Instead, lenders make the payments to FHA on behalf of the borrowers and the cost of the insurance is added to the borrower's loan balance.

A lender may choose either the assignment option or the coinsurance option when originating the loan. Under the assignment option, HUD will collect all the MIP, and the lender may assign the loan to HUD at the point that the loan balance equals the maximum HUD claim amount for the area. Under the coinsurance option, the lender may keep part of the MIP and forfeit the right to assign the case to HUD.

2.

Today's Reverse Mortgages

Types of Reverse Mortgages

There are three types of reverse mortgages:

- *single-purpose reverse mortgages*, offered by some state and local government agencies and nonprofit organizations;

- *federally-insured reverse mortgages*, known as Home Equity Conversion Mortgages (HECMs) and backed by HUD; and

- *proprietary reverse mortgages*, private loans that are backed by the companies that develop them

Single-purpose reverse mortgages are the least expensive option. They are not available everywhere and can be used for only one purpose, which is specified by the government or nonprofit lender. For example, the lender might say the loan may be used only to pay for home repairs, improvements, or property taxes. Most homeowners with low or moderate income can qualify for these loans.

HECMs and proprietary reverse mortgages may be more expensive than traditional home loans, and the upfront costs can be higher. That's important to consider, especially if you plan to stay in your home for just a short time or borrow a small amount. HECM loans are widely available, have no income or medical requirements, and can be used for any purpose.

Before applying for a HECM, you must meet with a counselor from an independent government-approved housing counseling agency. Some lenders offering proprietary reverse mortgages also require counseling. The counselor is required to explain the loan's costs and financial implications, and possible alternatives to a HECM, such as government and nonprofit programs or a single-purpose or proprietary reverse mortgage.

The counselor should also be able to help you compare the costs of different types of reverse mortgages and tell you how different payment options, fees, and other costs affect the total cost of the loan over time. You can visit HUD for a list of counselors or call the agency at 1-800-569-4287. Most counseling agencies charge around $150 for their services. The fee can be paid from the loan proceeds.

How much you can borrow with a HECM or proprietary reverse mortgage depends on several factors, including your age, the type of reverse mortgage you select, the appraised value of your home, and current interest rates. HUD has created a helpful table called the Principal Limit Factors, or PLFs, which explain these factors.

In general, the older you are, the more equity you have in your home, and the less you owe on it, the more money is available to you.

The HECM allows choice among several payment options. You can select:

- a "term" option – fixed monthly cash advances for a specific time.

- a "tenure" option – fixed monthly cash advances for as long as you live in your home.

- a line of credit that lets you draw down the loan proceeds at any time in amounts you choose until you have used up the line of credit.

- a combination of monthly payments and a line of credit.

You can change your payment option any time for about $20.

HECMs generally provide bigger loan advances at a lower total cost compared with proprietary loans. But if you own a higher-valued home, you may get a bigger loan advance from a proprietary reverse mortgage. So if your home has a higher appraised value and you have a small mortgage, you may qualify for more funds.

Loan Features

Reverse mortgage loan advances are not taxable, and generally don't affect your Social Security or Medicare benefits. You retain the title to your home, and you don't have to make monthly repayments. The loan must be repaid when the last surviving borrower dies, sells the home or no longer lives in the home as a principal residence, provided there is equity remaining in the home. If there is, the estate can sell the house and direct the funds. If there is negative equity, the estate walks away with no debt to the lender.

In the HECM program, a borrower can live in a nursing home or other medical facility for up to 12 consecutive months before the loan must be repaid.

If you're considering a reverse mortgage, be aware that:

- Lenders generally charge an origination fee, a mortgage insurance premium (for federally-insured HECMs), and other closing costs. The lender sometimes sets these fees and costs, although currently the law caps origination fees for HECM reverse mortgages. In the past some lenders charged service fees during the term of the mortgage, but the interest rate now includes these.

- The amount you owe on a reverse mortgage typically grows over time because you are not making payments. Interest accrues on the outstanding balance and added to the amount you owe each month, so your total debt increases as the loan funds are advanced to you and interest on the loan accrues.

- Although some reverse mortgages have fixed rates, most have variable rates tied to a financial index (e.g. the 1-month or 1-year LIBOR) which is likely to change with market conditions.

- Be aware that reverse mortgages can use up all or some of the equity in your home, and leave fewer assets for you and your heirs. Most reverse mortgages have a "non-recourse" clause, which prevents you or your estate from owing more than the value of your home when the loan becomes due or the home is sold. If you or your heirs want to retain ownership of the home, you usually must repay the loan in full. However, the heirs may be allowed to retain the home at 95% of fair market value versus having to pay the loan balance if that balance is greater than the home value.

- Because you retain title to your home, you are responsible for property taxes, insurance, utilities, fuel, maintenance and other expenses. If you don't pay property taxes, carry homeowner's insurance, or maintain the condition of your home, your loan may become due and payable.

- Because you are not paying mortgage payments, you may not deduct interest on reverse mortgages on your income tax return until the loan is paid off in part or whole. However, if a homeowner elects to make payments during the course of the loan, payments made during a particular calendar year may be tax deductible. You should consult a tax professional in your area regarding this matter. The interest is deferred until payments are made; whether those payments are partial payments or a payment in full. For example, if a homeowner elects to make regular or periodic payments in a given year those payments would be eligible for a calculation of how much interest was paid and what could be deductible in a given tax year.

Sample Loan Scenarios

Below are some sample loan scenarios to give you an idea how much money you may be able to receive under different loan programs and circumstances.

Getting a Good Deal

If you're considering a reverse mortgage, shop around. Compare your options and the terms various lenders offer. Learn as much as you can about reverse mortgages before you talk to a counselor or lender. That can help inform the questions you ask, which could lead to a better deal.

- If you want to make a home repair or improvement – or if you need help paying your property taxes – find out if you qualify for any low-cost single-purpose loans in your area. Area Agencies on Aging (AAAs) generally know about these programs. To find the nearest agency, visit www.eldercare. gov or call 1-800-677-1116. Ask about "loan or grant programs for home repairs or improvements," or "property tax deferral" or "property tax postponement" programs, and how to apply.

- All HECM lenders must follow HUD rules. And while the mortgage insurance premium is the same from lender to lender, most loan costs, including the origination fee, interest rate, closing costs and servicing fees vary among lenders.

- If you live in a higher-valued home, you may be able to borrow more with a proprietary reverse mortgage, but the more you borrow, the higher your costs. The best way to see key differences between a HECM and a proprietary loan is to do a side-by-side comparison of costs and benefits. Many HECM counselors and lenders can give you this important information.

- No matter what type of reverse mortgage you're considering, understand all the conditions that could make the loan due and payable. Ask a counselor or lender to explain the Total Annual Loan Cost (TALC) rates: they show the projected annual average cost of a reverse mortgage, including all the itemized costs.

Be Wary of Sales Pitches

Some companies may offer you goods or services, like home improvement services, and then suggest at a reverse mortgage as an easy way to pay for them. If you decide you need what's being offered, shop around before deciding on any particular vendor. Keep in mind that the total cost of the product or service is the price the seller quotes plus the costs – and fees – to obtain the reverse mortgage.

Some who offer reverse mortgages may pressure you to buy other financial products, like an annuity or long- term care insurance. Resist that pressure. You don't have to buy any products or services to get a reverse mortgage (except to maintain the adequate homeowners or hazard insurance that HUD and lenders require). Sellers of financial instruments may not legally originate reverse mortgages due to possible conflicts of interest. In fact, in some situations it's illegal to require you to buy any other products to get a reverse mortgage.

The bottom line: If you don't understand the cost or features of a reverse mortgage or any other product offered to you – or if there is pressure or urgency to complete the deal – walk away and take your business elsewhere. Consider seeking the advice of a family member, friend or someone else you trust.

Your Right to Cancel

With most reverse mortgages, you have at least three business days after closing to cancel the deal for any reason, without penalty. To cancel, you must notify the lender in writing. First cancel by fax or email to get the process started, then follow up with a letter by certified mail, and ask for a return receipt. That will allow you to document what the lender received and when. Keep copies of your correspondence and any enclosures. After you cancel, the lender has 20 days to return any money you've paid up to then for the financing.

You also have the same right to cancel if you have use a reverse mortgage to purchase a home (a so-called "reverse for purchase" transaction). When selling a property with a reverse for purchase buyer, the seller must attest to the fact that the buyer may cancel the purchase at any time and without any cause.

Tighter Rules on Reverse Mortgages

Seniors shopping for a reverse mortgage will find the rules for these loan products are getting tighter. That means borrowing costs are increasing and loan amounts are shrinking. And some cash-strapped people may find it tougher to qualify for a loan. One major change is the merger of the Standard and the lower-cost Saver programs. On October 1, 2013 HUD combined these products. Borrowers will now receive about 15% less in proceeds compared with the Standard product, but they will get more than with the previous Saver product, says Peter Bell, president of the National Reverse Mortgage Lenders Association.

The merged product charges 0.5% for an upfront mortgage insurance premium, compared with the Saver's 0.01% and the Standard's 2%. However, some seniors may get hit with a higher 2.5% upfront premium if they take more than 60% of the proceeds during the loan's first year.

If you need to take more than 60%, you can still get the loan, but the insurance premium will be higher. The annual premium of 1.25% of the loan amount remains the same.

A reverse mortgage allows seniors 62 or older to tap into a portion of their home equity. The loan does not have to be repaid until the homeowner dies, sells the house or moves out for at least 12 months.

Nearly all reverse mortgages are insured by the Federal Housing Administration (FHA). With the Home Equity Conversion Mortgage, or HECM, the government's mortgage insurance account pays the lender if the house sells for less than the loan balance. When the loan comes due, the homeowner and/or her estate will never owe more than the worth of the home.

HUD made these changes to strengthen the mortgage insurance fund, which was suffering from a struggling housing market and a growing number of projected defaults by borrowers. As housing prices dropped, lenders often could not recoup the full amount of the loans when they came due.

HUD also has asked Congress for about $1.7 billion to shore up the fund.

Another one of the new rules that went into effect on October 1, 2013 limits how the proceeds can be taken by a borrower within the first year of the loan closing. "Previously, you were able to take 100% of the available proceeds on day one," says Lori Trawinski, senior strategic policy adviser for the AARP Public Policy Institute. Now, in the first year the borrower can generally take no more than 60% of the total proceeds they are eligible to receive. The reason for the new limit is that borrowers taking all proceeds upfront were more likely to use up the money early on.

Often those borrowers were left without enough cash later on to pay property taxes and homeowners insurance, and the loans went into default. Obviously loans with a larger upfront draw carry larger risks.

An exception to the 60% limit, however, covers the scenario where the amount of "mandatory obligations" plus 10% of the maximum allowable proceeds is larger than 60% of the proceeds. Mandatory obligations include the upfront insurance premium, the loan origination fee and money needed to pay off a current mortgage. Borrowers who take more than 60% will pay the higher upfront insurance premium of 2.5%.

For example, say a borrower with a home value of $200,000 qualifies for a $100,000 loan. The first-year draw is $60,000. If the borrower has mandatory obligations of $20,000, the proceeds will cover those costs, and he can take the $40,000 balance in cash in the first year. He will pay an upfront premium of $1,000, or 0.5% of the home value. If his mandatory obligations instead are $70,000, the borrower can draw up to $80,000—$70,000 to cover the mandatory obligations plus 10% of the total loan, which is $10,000. This borrower will pay an upfront premium of 2.5%, or $5,000. Generally, borrowers who go this route are paying off a forward mortgage, but the upfront premium will generally arises in reverse for purchase as well.

Borrowers can take proceeds as a line of credit or monthly payments, and they will pay an adjustable interest rate. After the first year, the borrower can take the balance of available proceeds.

Those who desire a fixed interest rate can take a lump sum payment at closing. But the one-time lump sum is subject to the 60% and mandatory obligations limitations. You can't come back for more. In other words, if you qualify to take up to 60% in proceeds the first year, that's all you'll get.

New Hurdles to Qualify

For the first time, potential borrowers will need to undergo a financial assessment to determine whether they can afford to pay property taxes and homeowners insurance over the life of the loan. **Assessments were due to begin on January 13, 2014, but the financial**

assessment rule had yet to go into effect at the time this book went to print.

About 57,600 borrowers, or 9.8%, defaulted because of taxes and insurance in mid-2012, up from 8.1% in mid-2011, according to HUD. A borrower goes into default when he does not pay property taxes and insurance—a requirement of the loan.

AARP's Trawinski says such costs can be a hardship for some homeowners, particularly in states like New York, that have hefty property taxes, or in coastal states, such as Florida, with expensive insurance costs because of hurricane and flooding risks.

A borrower in default gets 24 months to become current on unpaid charges, and if he can't, he could lose his home if the lender forecloses.

Bell says lenders will scrutinize sources of income and assets as well as credit history. Some borrowers will be required to set aside part of the loan in an escrow account to pay future bills. Borrowers who clearly are able to cover those costs won't have to put cash aside.

Because the set-aside may need to last for 20 years or more, the amount could be very large. For some, the proceeds may end up paying only loan expenses, taxes and insurance—but covering those costs could enable the senior to stay in the home. And it would free up cash in a retiree's budget to pay for other expenses, says Michael

Kitces, Director of Research at Pinnacle Advisory Group in Columbia, Md.

A senior could be denied a reverse mortgage if the financial assessment shows he cannot pay insurance and taxes and have enough cash left to live on. Thus seniors who are strapped for cash may be cut out of the reverse mortgage market, says Trawinski.

Affluent borrowers are likely to pass the financial assessment, but many may see little appeal in a reverse mortgage now that the Saver has been eliminated. Because the Saver had ultra-low costs, some borrowers used it to extend the life of their investment portfolio by tapping the credit line during a market downturn, giving their stocks time to recover.

"Spending a few more thousand dollars upfront isn't a deal killer, but it takes a little value off the strategy," Kitces says. (Source: Kiplinger.com.)

Non-Borrowing Spouse Changes

HUD has issued changes to the status of non-borrowing spouses (NBS) of borrowers who order their FHA loan number after August 4, 2014. A non-borrowing spouse is one whose name is not included on the loan, usually because they are under the age of 62.

Lower proceeds out on the HECM loan will probably result since FHA uses the youngest borrower or NBS to calculate the potential loan amount.

For this type of HECM loans, the NBS will be able to remain in the homes, provided they are married to the borrower at the time of closing and establish, within 90 days of the death of the last surviving HECM mortgagor, legal ownership or another ongoing legal right to remain in the home securing the HECM loan. They also must take responsibility for meeting all of the obligations of the HECM mortgagor.

3.

Myths and Misconceptions of Reverse Mortgage

There are so many myths and misconceptions regarding reverse mortgages, we could write a book just on that subject alone! If you ask ten people to explain what a reverse mortgage is and how it works, you may get ten different answers. While some of that information may be correct, you should satisfy yourself when it comes to learning about something as important as a reverse mortgage.

Myths and Misconceptions

Here are just a few of the myths and misconceptions floating around:

- **The bank will own my home.** In a survey of people who worried about a reverse mortgage, this ranked as the top subject. Here's the honest truth: even with a reverse mortgage, you keep the ownership of your home. The bank or other lender cannot claim the right to your home, and it cannot foreclose on your home (as long as you keep up with the taxes and insurance payments). Part of the misinformation about this myth comes from the fact that many mortgage borrowers choose to sell their homes to pay off the loan when they move. In this way, the reverse mortgage behaves as a forward or traditional mortgage. It is a mortgage. You own the home the lender holds a financial interest.

- **I won't have any estate left for my heirs.** If you have anything left when you die, you have an estate for your heirs.

However, if you spent all of your money on collecting Hummel figurines and gave everything else to a local nonprofit organization, then you won't have an estate left. Many seniors are worried that a reverse mortgage will be keeping them from leaving any property or money for their children and grandchildren. Here is the bottom line: it is up to you to decide how to pay off your loan. YOU decide who you want to leave your estate to. If, after you die, you still owe money on the loan, it will be up to your heirs to decide the best way to handle the balance due.

- **My credit is so bad I will never qualify for a reverse mortgage.** It is no secret that the economy has been terrible for a long time. And because of it, many people have fallen behind on payments and other obligations, and that has had a negative impact on their credit report. However, even if you have bad credit, you will not be turned down for a reverse mortgage unless you are in an active bankruptcy or you have previously defaulted on an FHA-insured loan. Certain time constraints may apply to no-FHA foreclosures and short sales. But your credit report has no impact on whether or not you are approved for a reverse mortgage. Your mortgage company will run a credit report, but only to see if you have any outstanding debts owed to the government. If you do, that still will not prevent the reverse mortgage from being approved, but you will most likely have to settle the government debt before using the loan proceeds for anything else.

- **I have too many bills.** Another misconception is that you have to be debt free in order to be approved for a reverse mortgage. The only requirements are that you must be a homeowner and the property must be your primary residence. Beyond that, nothing else really matters. So, if you still have a few car payments, leftover orthodontist bills, the new roof you had to put on last year, etc., don't let those things keep you from moving forward with a reverse mortgage.

- **I am not desperate and destitute.** Many years ago, mainly seniors with serious financial difficulties applied for reverse mortgages. In today's world, however, someone applying for a reverse mortgage may be doing so out of "want," and not out of "need." If you, like most people, would enjoy the peace of mind that comes from having a financial cushion, then a reverse mortgage may work very well for you.

Mistakes to Avoid

You need to do your homework before you rush out and sign on the dotted line of the first reverse mortgage application presented to you. As with everything else in life, it is worth your time and effort to do everything you possibly can ahead of time to avoid mistakes down the road.

Here are some tips to help you avoid mistakes with a reverse mortgage:

- The first and most important step is to gather (and understand) all of the facts about a reverse mortgage. If you Google the term "reverse mortgage" on the Internet, you'll get thousands and thousands of results. Try not to become overwhelmed by the sheer amount of information out there. Your best bet is to speak with an experienced reverse mortgage professional who can help you decide which type of a package is best suited for your individual needs and plans. Ask for references, and don't be afraid to ask any questions you may have before you sign. The wrong program can end up costing you and your spouse thousands of dollars in interest and fees. Listen to your specialist, a professional there to educate you.

- Do not wait too long; there is no such thing as the "perfect time" to get a reverse mortgage. While it is okay to wait until you are a little older (and will be able to access more money), if the timing seems right and your trusted mortgage counselor says "it's time," don't delay. Even one-quarter to one-half percent more in interest rate will mean higher fees and less money for you. If you wait, you take the risk that the federal government might make changes to the program which could result in the loan being less advantageous to you.

4.

True Story!

I want to share some stories with you about actual borrowers. These are all true stories gathered from our loan originators as examples of people who have benefitted from a reverse mortgage. After the stories I will share some loan scenarios which will show you how much money you could borrow with a reverse mortgage, depending on age, loan programs and home values.

Borrower Stories

There was a sweet couple, Joe and Jo (yes, it IS true), ages 92 and 86, who wanted to obtain funds to enlarge their kitchen. She loved to cook. He loved to eat the fruits of her labor! They had a very narrow galley kitchen. When she bent over to use the oven, her rear end touched the cabinet behind her. I was so very impressed with a couple the ages of these two individuals wanting to really LIVE as long as they were alive and with her interest in continuing to hone her lifelong love of cooking. - **Carol**

Sophie had just lost her husband of 54 years. The cost of his care had drained their savings, and without his pension and Social Security she was not able to support herself or her home. In addition, she was worried about her own health and who would care for her. Her only son lives in another country. Sophie sold her house and, with the equity, purchased a townhouse in a senior community. She then got a reverse mortgage with a line of credit option. She withdraws a small amount each month to cover her shortfall, but is happy and secure that the line of credit and the annual growth will cover any future emergency needs such as health care. - **Rick**

I helped a physician in the metro Atlanta area, Dr. A., almost five years ago. He had no real or specific need for additional funds; however, he feared what could be coming with the American economy in the years ahead. He simply wanted to have more of his assets in an easily and quickly accessible vehicle, rather than trapped in his home's equity. But he wanted to retain the home in which he was so very comfortable. - **Carol**

Robert was 93 and retired from a successful law career. He had one son who was happy and secure and wanted his father "to make his retirement the most fun it could be with his money." Robert and his son enjoyed a hobby together, professional dune buggy racing. Robert was still a race official and wanted to contribute as much as he could. The race community was his family. Robert used some of the equity in his home to buy a large recreational vehicle; now his son and he go to every race during the season. He was thrilled and had a safe place to retreat. He told me spending time with his son was almost more fun than watching the race. The son said seeing his dad so happy was priceless. - **Rick**

Jim is a 66-year-old long-haul truck driver forced into retirement due to health issues. He was about $170,000 negative when he short-sold his home. He faced a staggering tax bill due to debt forgiveness. He had a free and clear home in Central California and realized he had to move there as a year-round place to live. He had no money and was not yet collecting Social Security Income. He was able to use a reverse mortgage to pay off his debts and have a fair amount available to him next year under the 60/40 rule. Here is a man who probably delivered groceries to my local store that is finally able to relax and get his life back in order. This loan program virtually saved Jim's financial life. - **Phil**

Al had his home completely paid for but was having a commercial loan called due by the bank. With the implementation of the reverse mortgage, he was able to save his business and still have his home to continue enjoying for himself and his family. - **Carol**

I received a call from a traditional mortgage broker asking me if I could help her aunt who was in foreclosure. She had a sale date two months away, and she had no loan programs in her arsenal for which her aunt, 83, qualified. Aunt Diane's house was worth more than $800,000 and she was about to lose it for $34,000 in back taxes. Her family didn't have the financial resources to help. Diane was competent but had health issues because of recent hip surgery and following complications. Diane wasn't very organized; she got into financial trouble and was too embarrassed to tell her family. The house had no insurance or heat. We got all the minor repairs made, and got her line of credit reverse mortgage funded with a week to spare. Her minor debts were paid off, taxes made current, heating and air conditioning installed, and escrow established so taxes and insurance could be funded for the next 27 years if necessary. - **Rick**

Sue is a self-employed professional in a good position to retire with the exception of a near-$300,000 existing first mortgage. Principle and interest payments run in the $1700 per month range. Upon analysis of her home equity, Sue was about $25,000 short of qualifying for the reverse mortgage and taking out her original mortgage and payments. She decided to pull the funds from her retirement account and she qualified for the loan. She brought the funds to closing. Within 16 months of closing, she will have recovered the $25,000 and plans to begin retirement immediately. - **Phil**

Peter was a lifelong bachelor, 68, and retired from the Navy. He owned a modest house in California and lived a happy, modest retired life. His mother was 91 and lived near New Orleans. Hurricane Katrina completely destroyed her home along with everything she owned and left her injured and homeless. Peter picked up his mother and brought her back to California. The next two years were financially and emotionally draining for Peter. In addition to caring for himself and his mom, and work part-time to make ends meet, his home was showing needing maintenance, his 135,000-mileage car rarely worked well, and he was tired of being flat broke all the time. At this point his mother passed away and he did not have the money to pay for the kind of funeral he wanted. I was volunteering at the Senior Center, and the director brought Peter to meet me. We discussed how a reverse mortgage would work for him and his situation. He has no relatives to pass the house to. We set up a budget, got him counseling, and started the process for a tenured reverse mortgage with an initial draw to do repairs. I was honored to be invited to the services for his mother, and it was wonderful, complete with gumbo and a brass quintet. I explained the situation to title, processing and under-writing, and all hands put in the extra effort to get the loan com-pleted quickly. Peter received his initial draw check via FedEx. As he drove into town to deposit the check, his engine blew up and he actually coasted down the off-ramp and into a Ford dealership. He called me and told me the story and let me know he got the check ok. "Are you all right?" I asked, thinking I could give him a ride. "I am great!" He said. "I have a reverse mortgage, and I am about to get a new car." - **Rick**

I had a borrower, a single guy who had plenty of monthly income and plenty of assets. He knew none of his children would ever have any thought of moving back home. His plan for the pro-ceeds from his reverse mortgage was to create an education ac-count for his eight grandchildren. What an awesome use of the program and the funds derived from the loan! - **Carol**

Mrs. T was an 83-year-old lady living with one son on disability. She had a bank HELOC which came to final maturity last fall. (Many of these HELOCs have in the fine print that after a certain amount of time paying only minimum payments, the borrower must either refinance to principal & interest payments or pay it off). Mrs. T was one of those seniors for whom refinancing was simply not an option, so she was now looking at a big problem with her bank. I received a call from the banker for help, and the end result is that we paid off her bank HELOC, got many needed repairs done in her home, and gave her an extra $18,000 of credit line to draw on if she needs it. She has got another $700 a month to spend as she wishes and an emergency fund to boot! - **Dan**

Paul and his wife had a beautiful home valued in excess of $1 million and were enjoying a comfortable retirement. Paul continued to work as a consulting engineer to pay the small monthly mortgage payment. Then their single adult daughter was diagnosed with cancer, had to quit her job, and was facing foreclosure as well as mounting medical bills. At that point Paul and his wife got a reverse mortgage. With the lump sum proceeds, they paid off their small mortgage, the mortgage on their daughter's house as an "early inheritance," and some of the medical bills. This allowed Paul to work only occasionally, and focus on his daughter. The daughter's recovery was smoother because she had much less stress. Paul and his wife still had financial security because their income was more than comfortable, they still have two real estate assets (homes), and the main house had significant equity and appreciation. They felt through the entire process that this was an excellent financial strategy that would support the extended family as well as let them stay in their forever home. - **Rick**

> Louise, a 92-year-old widow, had been referred to me by her financial advisor. She owned a $580,000 home in California that was free of any liens. Louise had a $1 million life insurance policy that was still in effect, but the family was having a problem paying the yearly premiums. One of the solutions her financial advisor recommended was to take advantage of the HECM program which allowed them initial access to $324,800. With the line of credit growth rate compounding at approximately 4.4%, the reverse mortgage would provide the family insurance coverage for at least five more years. The reverse mortgage was put into place as a financial hedge and worked great until Louise passed away 18 months later. Accessing part of the equity in the home with the reverse mortgage allowed Louise and her family to make the insurance premium payments and keep the policy in effect so that the life insurance proceeds could be passed, tax free to her estate. - **Carlos**

If you talk to your local reverse mortgage specialist, you will hear more stories just like these.

Sample Loan Amounts

Below are sample loan scenarios using the PLF (Principal Limit Factor) tables in use at the time this book went to press. Your loan originator can give you current numbers, but these are a start. In the tables I am showing 12 loan scenarios, which cover 3 home equity values ($200k, $400k, $625k), for ages 65 and 85, for two loan types each. The loan types are an Adjustable Rate Mortgage based on LIBOR and a fixed-rate loan.

For example, the chart shows that a person age 65 with a $200,000 home who takes out an ARM can get $64,920 the first year, and $43,280 the second year. (Remember, with an ARM you can take 60% of the available funds in the first year, and the rest the second year.) If you take a fixed-rate loan, you can get about $108,000. If you are age 85, you can get $76,200 the first year and $50,800 the second year, or $127,000 on a fixed-rate.

	Age 65	Age 85
$200,000 Home		
LIBOR Year 1	64,920	83,880
LIBOR Year 2	43,280	55,920
LIBOR Total Funds	108,200	139,800
Fixed Rate Maximum	108,400	139,800
$400,000 Home		
LIBOR Year 1	129,840	167,750
LIBOR Year 2	86,560	111,840
LIBOR Total Funds	216,800	279,600
Fixed Rate Maximum	216,400	254,000
$625,000 Home		
LIBOR Year 1	203,037	262,335
LIBOR Year 2	135,358	174,889
LIBOR Total Funds	338,395	437,224
Fixed Rate Maximum	339,021	437,224

5.

Parents, Adult Children and Reverse Mortgages

How to Discuss a Reverse Mortgages with Your Senior Parents

If you have senior parents, are you comfortable speaking with them about their finances? Many families find that "money" talk is taboo, and everyone knows better than to bring up the subject. But, as it has been said many times, "communication is the key." If you don't communicate about those financial issues, there may be trouble on the horizon.

We have all seen movies and television shows where adult children try to have a coherent conversation with their parents about their monthly bills and ability to pay them. These shows are often sitcoms, with everything working out perfectly for everyone in the end. In the real world, however, adult children and their parents don't often see eye-to-eye when it comes to money matters. Here are some tips to help have a conversation with your adult parents about their finances without making everyone feel uncomfortable:

- Select a time that works best for everyone. Do not pick a time too close to their bedtime. You want their undivided attention, without one or both of them yawning and falling asleep in the middle of your conversation.

- Select a place that is not controversial. If you meet at their house, they may play the "It's my house and we'll go by my rules" card. If you meet at your house, they may feel as if you are bullying them. Pick a neutral location. Most libraries have small meeting rooms you can use at no cost. Or perhaps you can reserve a small private dining room at a local restaurant.

- Draft your "talking points" ahead of time, and give your parents a copy so neither party is blindsided by surprises.

- Make sure you have done your homework and researched the ABCs of reverse mortgages (and other options); be prepared to explain it slowly so they will understand all of their options.

- Have access to your reverse mortgage professional for any questions that may arise.

How Seniors Can Discuss a Reverse Mortgage with Their Adult Children

If you think you are uncomfortable speaking about reverse mortgages and finances with your parents, imagine how your parents must feel! However, it may actually be the senior parents who want to explore the possibility of a reverse mortgage, and they may be concerning about upsetting their children with their plans.

Here are some tips for parents who want to talk about their personal finances and a possible reverse mortgage with their adult children:

- Have a reverse mortgage professional there with you when you meet with your children.

- Come prepared to explain the facts about reverse mortgages, or have the reverse mortgage professional explain them. Too many people, including adult children, have their own idea of a reverse mortgage, and much of that information may not be true.

- Prepare ahead of time for any arguments or objections you feel you may hear from your children. After all, you raised them, and you know what strengths and weaknesses they will bring to the table. For example, is your daughter stubborn and not open to new ideas? If so, within a few minutes her body language will give away her true feelings on the topic!

- **Assure your adult children that they will not be losing their inheritance.** Again, once you are armed with the facts, figures and statistics, it will be easier to share with them.

- Pick a time that works for everyone. If your adult children work until late in the evening, refrain from wanting to meet as soon as they walk in the front door.

- Select a location that is non-threatening. Again, look for a neutral location.

Understanding Reverse Mortgages: The Pros and Cons

When it comes to helping an aging loved one with financial decisions, caregivers should take the time to make sure they all aspects of the transaction. One increasingly popular option for seniors is to use the equity from their home to increase their cash flow. Some seniors need to pay off old home equity loans; others have credit card debt that they would like to eliminate. Some senior parents need additional cash flow to pay in-home caregivers, and some need the money simply to be able to afford to pay their daily living expenses. Regardless of the reason, a reverse mortgage (also known as a Home Equity Conversion Mortgage) is a big decision for the senior, family members and caregivers.

Reverse mortgages have received a lot of press lately. NBC Nightly News, ABC, and CBS have all run stories. Of course, there are pros and cons to reverse mortgages, but interestingly enough, two large organizations support and advocate them, especially for seniors who need long-term care.

A study released by The National Council on the Aging (NCOA) shows that reverse mortgages can be used by over 13 million

Americans to pay for long-term care expenses at home, allowing many to remain independent and in their homes longer. The "Use Your Home to Stay at Home: Expanding the Use of Reverse Mortgages to Pay for Long Term Care" report, funded by the Centers for Medicare and Medicaid Services and the Robert Wood Johnson Foundation, also shows how reverse mortgages can alleviate financial pressure not only for individuals and families, but also for state Medicaid programs and the federal government.

Reverse Mortgage Pros

Reverse mortgages are backed and regulated by the federal government (HUD and FHA). Seniors age 62 and older are eligible for this federal program. A reverse mortgage is a "non-recourse loan," which means that the heirs of the seniors are not responsible for repaying the loan. In fact, a reverse mortgage is a loan that does not have to be repaid unless both homeowners (assuming a couple) leave the home permanently, or pass away. Depending on remaining equity, heirs may sell the property, pay off the loan and have net proceeds go to the estate. No monthly payments are required. The senior is the one who gets paid.

The money seniors receive from a reverse mortgage is tax free, and does not interfere with SSI or Medicare benefits. [In some cases such as SS Disability where recipients are restricted as to how much cash they can have on hand, it is wise to consult a professional.] For seniors having trouble making ends meet, the reverse mortgage can be a lifesaver.

Some seniors are using the extra cash to pay for in-home care, adult day care, prescription drugs, credit card debt, and make much-needed home repairs so that they can live safely and more comfortably.

When the reverse mortgage is used to pay off any existing liens, a new cash flow is created. Funds no longer going to payments become income.

Many seniors' homes have been saved from foreclosure by using their home equity to pay past-due property taxes, or to pay off current mortgages that have become unaffordable.

Prior to beginning processing for a reverse mortgage, seniors are required to attend a HUD counseling session designed to make sure the senior understands how the reverse mortgage works and to answer any questions. They speak with a trained counselor either over the phone or in person. A certificate, which ultimately must accompany the reverse mortgage application, is sent to the senior after the counseling session is completed.

Reverse Mortgage Cons

When considering a reverse mortgage, it is important that the senior plans on staying in their home for a few years. For those who are considering moving in the next year, it would be more appropriate to wait until the senior is living in the new home to move forward with the application process, or perhaps even consider using the reverse for purchase opportunity.

Closing costs are almost always factored into the loan, leaving very few, if any, out-of-pocket costs for seniors. Nevertheless, closing costs are still an issue, which means you should plan to stay in the home for more than a year.

If you are a caregiver for a senior parent who currently needs in-home care, the proceeds from a reverse mortgage can be extremely helpful. Reverse mortgage proceeds should not affect Medicare, Social Security, or Medicaid eligibility.

52 | Parents, Adult Children and Reverse Mortgages

6.

Are You Eligible?

Because a reverse mortgage is a tool to help seniors and based on equity in the home, eligibility requirements are fairly straightforward.

Borrower Requirements

Age Requirements

Borrower(s) must be 62 years of age or older. In the past a younger spouse could be treated as a non-borrowing spouse (NBS), that is, a spouse who is not on the loan. But new rules came out in August 2014 which address the danger if a reverse mortgage is taken out, the borrower then dies and the NBS now must move since the NBS is not on the loan.

Equity

The borrower must either own the home outright or have a significant amount of equity in the property. In other words, you should owe less than 40% of what your home is worth. Alternatively, borrowers could also bring cash to closing to increase their equity.

Primary Residence

Reverse mortgages are currently available for your primary residence only, not vacation properties or rentals. HUD-approved properties with two to four units are also eligible as long as one of the units is your primary residence.

Financial Resources to Cover Property Expenses

In the past no qualifying was necessary for a reverse mortgage. Now, in order to protect seniors from losing their home through foreclosure, seniors must prove they can afford to continue to pay property taxes, homeowner's insurance and other property expenses such as homeowner's association dues (if applicable).

If there is a question about your ability to pay those expenses you should discuss the situation with a qualified loan originator; if you truly have an issue, deposits or set-asides could be used to help you qualify.

No Federal Debt

You may not have any outstanding federal debt, such as monies owed to the IRS, at the time the loan closes. However, it may be possible to use funds from the reverse mortgage to pay off such debts in the closing process. In fact, it is not uncommon for seniors to refinance with a reverse mortgage to pay off tax liabilities, AND stop having to make house payments in the bargain.

Not in Bankruptcy

The borrower(s) must not be in the process of bankruptcy, AND must not be intending to enter bankruptcy. (Borrowers must sign a statement to this effect.) However, you may have gone through a bankruptcy previously as long as it has been discharged and as long as there was NOT a Federal loan, VA or FHA, discharged in the bankruptcy proceedings. If there was a federal loan discharged in the bankruptcy, then consult a local reverse mortgage consultant to see the length of time necessary to wait until a reverse mortgage can be originated.

Spousal Competency

Both borrowers must be mentally competent. In the event of a spouse deemed incompetent (from dementia or other causes), special requirements arise. In that case you should seek advice from a mortgage advisor in your area and preferably from an attorney also since a simple power of attorney may not be sufficient.

If the reverse mortgage is connected to a medical power of attorney, all the papers will need to be submitted with the application paperwork along with a letter from the doctor. The person who has power of attorney will also be involved with the counseling session. There is a place on the counseling certificate for the person acting under POA to sign and date.

Attorney Review of Trust

If your property is held in trust, it still may possible to take out a reverse mortgage. There are two strategies for doing this. Originally, borrowers would have to remove their property from the trust, originate the reverse mortgage, and then put the property back into the trust, and in certain cases this procedure is still followed. However, it is also possible with some lenders to get an attorney review of trust, and avoid removing the property from the trust. Expenses involved in each of these trust-related reverse mortgages may vary. If the reverse mortgage is connected to a trust, the all trust documents must be submitted with the application paperwork.

Property Requirements

FHA Appraisal, including Photos

An FHA-approved appraiser will need to appraise your property and will compare your property to comparable properties in your area to ascertain current market value. The appraisal will cover the size and layout of your home, as well as many other aspects such as location and upkeep. The appraisal report must contain photographs of your home so people viewing the appraisal can get a clear impression of your home.

Health and Safety, Repairs

If there are health or safety issues with your home including, for instance, worn-out shingles, missing caulk or paint, deteriorated siding; or All repairs need to be completed before you can close the loan. In short, your home should be in safe working order, with only minimal deferred maintenance items.

FHA Restrictions on Condos or Manufactured Homes

Besides single family homes and units containing two to four homes, it is possible to obtain a reverse tmortgage on condominiums and manufactured homes, with some restrictions. The FHA guidelines require that loans can only be made to FHA-approved condos or manufactured homes. For condos this means that the entire condo association, not your single unit, has been approved by FHA. Manufactured homes must not be mobile, and must be bolted down to appropriate concrete foundations, among other requirements.

7.

Plan Your Expenses

Expenses in Obtaining the Loan

FHA Appraisal

FHA requires an appraisal, as explained in the previous chapter. Appraisal fees vary by state but are typically between $450 and $575. This is a fee that must be paid up front.

Loan Origination Fee

Lenders may charge a loan origination fee, but this fee is regulated by FHA. On a reverse mortgage a lender can charge an origination fee up to $2,500 if your home is valued at less than $125,000. For homes valued at more than $125,000 lenders can charge 2% of the first $200,000 of value plus 1% of the amount over $200,000. HECM reverse mortgage origination fees are always capped at $6,000.

Third Party Charges

You will be charged closing costs from third parties such as title insurance companies, appraisers and inspectors. These companies are generally referred to as "settlement service providers," and all provide services needed to get your loan closed. These third-party services may include title search, title insurance, surveys, inspections, recording fees, mortgage taxes, credit checks and others.

Mortgage Insurance Premium

A HECM reverse mortgage is an FHA-insured loan. The reason the lender is willing to make the loan is because the lender is insured against loss by FHA. You will be charged an FHA mortgage insurance premium when the loan is originated. The mortgage insurance premium (MIP) guarantees that you will receive expected loan advances and enables this to be a non-recourse loan with the loan having no monthly payments. It is possible to finance the mortgage insurance premium (MIP) as part of your loan.

Servicing Fee

Servicing a loan is the process of receiving the payments every month, sending account statements to the borrower(s) and dispersing the monies to the investor. It may also include managing escrowed funds to pay real estate taxes and homeowners insurance. Lenders may charge a monthly fee capped at $30-$35 per month, depending on how the interest rate adjusts. And if there is a servicing fee, when the loan is originated the lender computes how much money is needed for servicing and reduces the amount you may borrow by that amount. Then each month the servicer is paid, and the borrower's loan balance is increased by the amount of the payment. To clarify, you are not paying it up this fee front. It is being added to your loan's outstanding balance each month. Some loan programs may not have a servicing fee but will include servicing in the interest rate charged, meaning you pay a slightly higher interest rate, but do not pay servicing as a separate fee.

Expenses While You Live In the Home

To have a successful reverse mortgage experience you should plan for the following expenses. However, it's interesting to note that these are all expenses you must plan for whether you have a reverse mortgage or not.

Property Taxes

You must continue to pay your annual property taxes, whether you have a reverse mortgage or not. If you do not stay current on property taxes your property may be foreclosed.

Homeowner's Insurance

Like other loans, your reverse mortgage will require you to keep an appropriate homeowner's insurance policy in place, to protect you and the lender, in the event of damage to the home.

Homeowner's Association Dues

You must be prepared to pay homeowner's association dues if you are in a neighborhood with an association. If you fail to stay current, the association can actually begin foreclosure proceedings against you, although that is rare.

Home Maintenance

When signing paperwork for your reverse mortgage you agree to maintain your property in safe working order. As seniors age, keeping up repairs can become more difficult. You should really have a plan in place for how you will maintain your property. This is important first and foremost for your safety, but also to protect the ongoing value of your home. Having worn carpet or older paint is one thing, but a small water leak can destroy a home over time and lead to health risks for the occupants.

8.

The Approval Process

The Steps to Approval

1) HECM Counselor & Financial Assessment

The first step in the process is to meet with an approved HECM counselor. The counselor is neither a loan originator nor an employee of a lender, but a trained counselor approved by HUD, whose job is to educate potential borrowers on the pros, cons and other details regarding reverse mortgages. You are required by HUD to communicate with the HECM counselor so you can be sure to understand the consequences of the loan as set out for you by a disinterested third party. Lenders are not allowed to take a loan application from you until after you have a certificate of counseling.

2) Meeting with Loan Advisor (Loan Originator)

Speaking to the counselor is the first formal step, but you may want to speak to a local loan originator before you go to counseling. The loan originator cannot take an application, but she can tell you about the loan process and the amounts involved; thus, they can help you decide, in a general way, if you would like to proceed.

If you are considering purchasing a home using a reverse mortgage, a loan advisor will be able to help you and your realtor or agent to understand how program works, what restrictions are in place, and the amount of loan for which you qualify (or amount of money needed to pre-qualify for a particular home).

Also, talking to a loan originator is free, but going to counseling does cost money, usually around $150. So starting with the loan officer to get a general idea, then spending the money for official counseling often makes the most sense.

3) Application

After you have decided what type of reverse mortgage you want and what amounts make sense for you, it's time to fill out the loan application. Your loan originator will sit down with you, ask you questions, and fill out the application for you. The loan originator will also give you a list of any documents you need to submit with the loan application. Although you must be at least 62 years old to take out a reverse mortgage, you can actually apply up to three months before you turn 62, as long as the loan does not close until the day after you turn 62.

4) Credit Report

Throughout the history of reverse mortgages the borrower's credit history was not a consideration. The qualification for the loan was based on the equity in the subject property. As long as there was sufficient equity in the property, a loan was possible. But in 2013 HUD announced new guidelines requiring a check of the borrower's credit history and finances. The credit report not only identifies federal and other liens on your property but also confirms your identity. The point of the credit check is to assure that borrowers have sufficient income or financial resources to pay property taxes and insurance payments, so that a loan would not go into foreclosure due to unpaid taxes or insurance.

At the time of writing this ruling has not yet been invoked. But your loan originator can tell you about the credit, if any, necessary to qualify. Again, the purpose of this qualification is to assure that seniors are not placed in a position to lose their home through foreclosure for nonpayment of taxes or insurance.

4a) Tax and Insurance Set Aside

If the credit history and financial assessment indicate that the borrower may have difficulty making property tax or insurance payments, it may be possible, or required, to set up an escrow account or set-aside account to provide money for those payments. The monies would be set aside from the loan closing, or added to the loan balance, and used by the servicer to make tax and insurance payments. If the monies are not set aside at the time of loan closing, the amount available to the borrower will probably be reduced to leave room in the loan for those payments to be added to the loan amount when the servicer makes those payments.

5) Processing

Once you and the loan originator have filled out the application and gathered supporting documents, the loan will go into processing.

In this stage the loan processor will enter your information into a computer system called an LOS, or Loan Origination System. The processor will double check the numbers and make sure they all make sense and that everything on the application is filled in and ready for review by the underwriter. The loan processor will also order the appraisal and title search.

6) Appraisal

The lender will order the appraisal, but you will be responsible for paying the cost of the appraisal. The appraisal will be done by a licensed, HUD-approved appraiser, who will come up with a value for your home as compared to other similar homes in your area, with adjustments up or down based on exact details of your home.

HUD has certain standards for the condition of your home, and if you have deficiencies or there are repairs necessary, the appraiser will call these out. Repairs impacting safety must be completed before the loan can be closed. For other repairs, you may be able to set money aside from the loan closing and have repairs made after the closing.

7) Loan Submission & Underwriting

Once your loan has been processed and you have all documents ready, the processor will submit the file to the lender for underwriting. Underwriting is the process of reviewing all details of the loan file to make sure the borrower qualifies for the loan, that all guidelines are met and that the loan complies with all laws. Depending on how busy the lender is, underwriting can take from one to several days.

An underwriter reviewing a file may give a conditional approval, meaning that the file can be approved if certain conditions, or stipulations, are met. That may require the loan originator or processor to request additional information or documentation from you.

8) Loan Approval

Once satisfied that the loan package is complete and that you meet the loan guidelines, the underwriter issues a final loan approval. Your loan originator and processor will be notified, and they will contact you to coordinate the closing.

9) Loan Closing

The loan closing consists of the parties going to the title company and signing the loan documents. The lender will prepare the closing documents ahead of time and send them to the title company. Your lender should also review the details of the transaction with you one last time before you sign the closing documents. Your loan originator should also reconfirm whether you need to bring any money to closing or if you will be getting cash out at closing.

Preparing for closing may take a few days from the time the loan is approved, giving time for the lender and title company to review any payoffs, payments, escrows and other details. Your lender and title company will also coordinate with you, with the closing held at a time and location that works best for you. It can occur at a title company but can also be done at your home or another convenient location.

10) Funds Dispersal

After your loan is closed you have a three-day "right of rescission" period, that is, three business days for you to decide you do not want the loan after all. The exception to the three-day rule is if you are using a HECM to purchase a home. There is no rescission period on a purchase transaction.

After the rescission period expires, the title company will disburse funds. If you had a previous mortgage it will be paid off, and if you are receiving funds they will be available to you.

It is recommended that borrowers utilizing a line of credit option take enough money at closing to cover 90 days of expenses.

9.

The Life of Your Reverse Mortgage

Your Loan Servicer

Once your loan closes, it will be managed by a loan servicer. With a traditional mortgage the servicer is the company that accepts payments and forwards them to the lender. In a reverse mortgage, no payments are required, but the servicer still tracks your loan balance. The loan servicer will also make sure that taxes are being paid and that the borrower continues to live in the home.

If you chose fixed monthly payments, your loan servicer will be the one to send those payments to you monthly and will begin making disbursements on the first day of the month.

Paying Off or Settling Your Loan

A "maturity event" occurs when the loan matures, that is, becomes due and payable. You do not need to make any payments during the life of the loan. However, once the last homeowner on title dies or moves out of the house for 12 consecutive months, a maturity event has occurred. The borrower, the borrower's heirs or the borrower's estate has up to 12 months to pay the loan off. The 12-month period is initially parceled out into a six-month period, with two separate 90-day extensions available if necessary and requested.

If contact is made with the servicer right away, usually it will give up to 12 months to the heirs to pay back the loan. Thus, when such a maturity event occurs, the homeowner, his heirs or his estate representative should notify the servicer. The borrowers still own the home and it can pass to the heirs as long as the loan is paid off.

A reverse mortgage is a non-recourse loan, meaning that if the homeowners owe more than the home is worth they are not responsible for the negative balance. However, if the heirs want to keep the home they may have to pay off the entire loan balance, or alternatively, let the lender take over the house, and then buy it from the lender at market value. The exception to this rule is if the original homeowner has conveyed title to the heirs. Then the heirs may pay off the loan at the lesser of the loan balance or 95% of the appraised value of the property. Financially, this is another great advantage of the reverse mortgage.

10.

HECM for Purchase

The next chapter will discuss advanced strategies for reverse mortgage, the most interesting of which is buying a home using a reverse mortgage. It's such a hot topic that I decided to give it its own chapter.

What Is It?

The primary feature of a reverse mortgage is that it allows you to have a loan on your home without making payments on that loan. You may or may not get cash out of your home when you refinance with a reverse mortgage, but you have no payments either way.

HECM for purchase is the strategy of using a reverse mortgage to purchase a home but have no mortgage payments.

How Is It Possible?

All reverse mortgages are possible because you have equity in your home. If you owe $50,000 on a $200,000 home the lender is willing to refinance your home and allow you to make no payments until you move out or sell the home because of your equity in the home. The lender knows you can pay them back out of the proceeds from selling the home.

A HECM for purchase is exactly the same thing, but you are purchasing a new or an existing home and making a down payment

78 | HECM for Purchase

that provides your equity position. In the example above, if you owe $50,000 on a home worth $200,000, the value of your equity is $150,000. So if you put $150,000 down on a $200,000 home it puts the lender in the same situation.

How Does This Help Me?

The two major benefits of a HECM for purchase involve living expenses and lifestyle.

The primary benefit of purchasing your home with a reverse mortgage is having no mortgage payments. This reduces your living expenses compared to having a payment. If you are scaling down from a larger home, you can achieve the same result by purchasing a home for cash, but you are limited by how much cash you have.

The second benefit of a HECM for purchase is that it increases your buying power, allowing you to purchase more home than you could afford if paying all cash. Or it can allow you to purchase the same amount of home but keep some of your cash available. For example, if you sold your family home and had $200,000 cash left after expenses, you could buy another home for $200,000 and have no payments. But using a HECM for purchase, you could buy a home for $375,000 or more, with the same cash. Or you could buy a $200,000 home, with a little over $100,000 down and keep almost $100,000 in savings. Remember, cash is king!

Depending on the neighborhood where you want to purchase your home, being able to afford a little more home might allow you to be in a nicer or safer part of town, or might allow you to have some features you might not have otherwise. It could also allow you to have cash to make renovations to make the home work for you.

There is another important benefit for some people, and that is saving transaction costs. Without the HECM for purchase, a senior could sell her current home, purchase a new home with a mortgage (if they could qualify) and then refinance into a reverse mortgage to avoid payments. The HECM for Purchase combines the standard mortgage and HECM refinance into one step. In fact, it was HUD noticing a trend of people doing just this that led to the HECM for purchase.

Are There Restrictions?

A HECM for purchase can be used for properties with one to four units as long as the borrower lives in one of the units. A HECM for purchase may not be used for a boarding house, a cooperative condo unit, a bed and breakfast or non-qualifying manufactured homes. See your loan advisor for details.

Who Can Help Me With a HECM For Purchase?

Any loan originator who can do a HECM loan can do a HECM for purchase, but you should look for someone with specific experience with the HECM for purchase since that type of reverse mortgage is subtly different from a standard HECM. A loan originator doing his first HECM for purchase will have a learning curve and will definitely encounter issues. When you are purchasing a home the last thing you want is delays that affect your closing date! Therefore, ask your prospective loan originator directly whether she has performed HECM's for purchase before and how many.

HECMs for purchase do have some tighter controls and rules. For example, a short sale or foreclosure triggers a 3-year waiting period before the former homeowner can be approved for a HECM for purchase, whereas no such waiting period exists for HECM for refinance. Talk with your loan originator for the details.

11.
Advanced Strategies

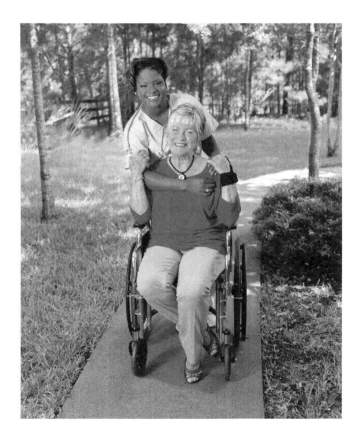

Historically, many people who took out a reverse mortgage had an urgent need for the money. It might be to pay taxes or another debt, or it might be for living expenses or health care. But they took out the loan because of an immediate need. Now that reverse mortgages have been around a while, people have realized that there are other uses for the funds and other strategies for using a reverse mortgage.

Protect Investments with a HECM

One of the most surprising strategies I have heard of is one that a lot of financial planners are using. The idea is to take out a reverse mortgage to protect other retirement investments and to lengthen the benefits you get from them those investments.

Your first thought may be that people who have other investments (money in mutual funds, for example) will not need a reverse mortgage. But we have just lived through "The Great Recession," and one of the lessons we learned is that the value of our investments is not always going to go up. Sometimes they go down. Sometimes they go way down! But the more our investments go down, the more likely it is that they will eventually come back up. Maybe not all the way back up, but back up to some degree. That is where the reverse mortgage comes in.

By taking out a reverse mortgage against your home, specifically an ARM, you have a line of credit to draw against if you need the money. You don't even need to take out much when you set up the line, just leave the line available for future use. If there comes a time when your investments are down, but you need to take out money, you can pull funds from the reverse mortgage. Then in the future when the market is better, you can sell some of your mutual funds and repay the reverse mortgage. The benefit is, you had access to money when you needed it, but you sold your securities at the most advantageous time. At least you were not forced to sell them at the worst time! And don't forget that there were no taxes on the funds borrowed.

The trick here is to use the ARM reverse mortgage because it will provide you a line of credit for future draws, and you can choose to pay it down at any time, or make no payments, as you wish.

ARM - Credit Line Growth

There is another important thing to remember about the ARM reverse mortgage. When you set up the reverse mortgage, your property is appraised, your age is considered, and according to the Principal Limit Factor tables the maximum amount you can draw is set. However, the assumption is that your home will appreciate, so there is also a schedule of how the amount you can draw increases over time. That is set at the time you take your loan, so even if the value of your home goes down, the amount you can take on your line goes up. This is a powerful feature of the ARM reverse mortgage.

ARM - Line Appreciation

If your home appreciates more than scheduled it is also possible that you will be able to refinance your reverse mortgage and reset the maximum amount you can draw and your appreciation schedule.

Deferring Social Security Draws

Another advanced reverse mortgage option is to defer taking Social Security at an early age since an earlier withdrawal carries a penalty that reduces the amount of your monthly check. If income is needed to retire or to supplement a borrower's monthly cash flow, the reverse mortgage term or tenure payments can be set up to supplement the money that an early Social Security draw might receive. And by deferring the start of Social Security payments, the person will receive payments which can be significantly larger over their lifetime than if they had begun Social Security payments earlier.

Buy-Out Spouse for Divorce Settlement

It's sad but true that more seniors are divorcing than in years past. Probably as our lives get longer, and we remain in reasonably better health than seniors might have in years past, people are realizing there is no reason to stay in a dysfunctional relationship. The problem is, without liquid funds a divorce is difficult to finance. Often the main asset is the family home. You can always sell the home and divide the assets, but then neither spouse gets to keep the family home.

A reverse mortgage can be a solution that provides liquidity to one spouse while allowing the other spouse to keep the home. And who knows, if they decide to get back together, as sometimes happens, they still have their home.

Buy-Out Business Partner

A similar type of divorce is the business divorce, or splitting up of business partners. If you have a partner and are lucky enough to have a business last into your senior years, you should be proud of that accomplishment. But eventually, if you aren't selling the business or giving it to kids, one of the partners will have to drop out.

Again, a reverse mortgage can be a source of equity to facilitate a partner buy out, to allow the business to proceed and to give one partners a viable exit. The partner who retains the business receives funds from their home and then takes over the business without selling their home to do it. Because they own the entire business, their profit share should be larger, and they can consider paying down the reverse mortgage.

Purchase Investment Property

This is not a real estate investment book, so I won't give advice about when it's a good idea to buy investment properties and when it's not. But if you do believe the real estate market is on the rise, you can use funds from a reverse mortgage to purchase investment properties. You can't use a HECM for purchase to buy an investment property, but you can use a reverse mortgage to get cash out of your primary residence (if you have enough equity) and you can use that cash toward the down payment on investment properties (although this strategy may involve higher risk than most are comfortable with). Be sure you have experience or great advisors. Preferably both.

Purchase Vacation/Second Home

Similar to an investment property, you cannot use a HECM for purchase to buy a vacation home, but you can use a reverse mortgage on your primary residence to raise money for a second home or vacation home.

The reverse mortgage can help you raise cash. In addition, taking away your house payments (if you still have them) frees up money in your budget.

As with all real estate transactions, you should be quite knowledgeable about your market before you jump into any of these transactions. A reverse mortgage can facilitate one of these transactions by freeing up cash, but it can also get you in trouble if you are attempting to purchase more than you can afford.

Life Insurance Strategies

Some reverse mortgage strategies involve life insurance. For example, if you are worried about using up the equity in your home, you can use some of the proceeds from a reverse mortgage to purchase life insurance. The reverse mortgage prevents the homeowner from having payments, and the life insurance policy will insure that there are funds for funerals or other purposes when the insured passes away.

Long-term care insurance has been a topic of discussion for years, but it seems to be falling out of favor. The problem is that premiums are becoming unbearably high, thus posing the problem that those premiums may gobble up too much equity before the insured even becomes ill.

A licensed insurance agent is the best person to see about insurance options and strategies. The only caution I would give is this: Be sure you understand any insurance strategy you undertake. Insurance agents only make money when they sell insurance. If you do not understand a strategy, you should not agree to it. But a reverse mortgage can be used alongside an insurance strategy.

Pay for In-Home Care

Another use of proceeds from a reverse mortgage is in-home care. Many seniors would prefer to stay in their home and not move to a rest home. Similarly, some save money by receiving care in their own home as opposed to moving to a rest home. A reverse mortgage can be part of a strategy to keep a senior in her home, and have money to pay for in-home care, saving money over institutional care.

Create an Annuity Stream

I have to be very careful with this one. An annuity is a stream of payments. Many insurance companies sell annuities. Depending on the terms, they can be a useful tool, or they can be a bad idea. Certainly, if a loan originator ever suggests you should use a reverse mortgage to generate cash and then use the cash to purchase an annuity, you should be very skeptical. That loan originator is probably making money from the sale of such annuities. However, a reverse mortgage can be structured to behave like an annuity; that is, it can be set up to give you a stream of payments. Your financial plans may include a stream of payments, which could be perfectly reasonable for you and a good use of a reverse mortgage.

Charitable Contributions

Making charitable contributions to schools, museums, or non-profit organizations after you have passed is all well and good. But it leaves the donor only imaging that they will be appreciated. If a senior would like to see the look on someone's face, or see the changes their donation will make, accessing funds through a reverse mortgage does allow them to make that donation while alive to see the result.

College Tuition for Grandchildren

Like donating to a museum or charity, providing college tuition while you are alive allows the donor to see the good they are doing. In fact, when your grandkids become college age they need the help when they need it, not at some future date after you pass away. A reverse mortgage can be a way to make those funds available to help with college expenses when they occur.

Conclusions

The reverse mortgage has been around for decades and has been used to help thousands of seniors improve retirement finances.

Programs have changed over time, in 2013, and again in August of 2014, but they still offer borrowers financial solutions to improve their retirement.

Reverse mortgages can be used in emergency situations to help seniors who are on the verge of losing their homes, but they can also be used as a strategic investment tool for seniors with many assets.

You owe it to yourself to understand this financial tool and consider whether it should be part of your retirement plan.

A1.

Planning for Your Retirement Years

Your Planning Considerations

Where does the time go? If you are like most people, you look back over your life and before you know it, retirement is staring you in the face. Whether it has officially arrived for you or is on the horizon and will be here soon, unless you have been planning for that stage of your life, you may found yourself in a "worry zone." But rest assured, no matter how much (or how little) retirement planning you have done over the years, the day will come when it happens, and you want to be able to face it and say "bring it on!"

Of course, if you have been able to save a couple million dollars and have lots of real estate holdings, stocks and bonds, etc., when retirement arrives you won't even break a sweat. But for the millions of people across the United States that have not been that fortunate, retirement can seem like a real nightmare. And that is where a reverse mortgage can be a great tool!

In the next 25 years, one in five Americans will be over 65. That's a lot of people who need to get to work during the next 10 to 15 years on an organized and realistic retirement plan. Make sure you have a plan so your retirement wishes come true.

Consider these facts from the United States Department of Labor:

- Fewer than half of Americans have calculated how much they need to save for retirement.

- In 2012, 30 percent of private industry workers with access to a defined contribution plan (such as a 401(k) plan) did not participate.

- The average American spends 20 years in retirement.

(Top Ten Ways to Prepare for Retirement, dol.gov/ebsa/publications/10_ways_to_prepare.html.)

Where do you fit on the "retirement" scale? Are you one of those people who have been saving and investing religiously over the past thirty years or more? Or are you a little nervous because, through no fault of your own, your retirement planning kept getting delayed over and over?

Assuming you have a little time before retirement arrives, try this:

- Keep track of all expenses for one month. Include everything: food, gas, utility bills, credit card bills, entertainment, etc.

- After one month, review your list (trying not to faint) and think about how you will live without your paycheck.

Will you realistically be able to keep the same level of comfort that you are enjoying at the present time? If things are looking a little tight, now is the time to start paying down debts, keeping an eye on your spending and look for creative ways to reduce spending and save money at the same time.

Where Are You Going to Live?

There is another very important question to ask yourself: Where are you going to live? Are you planning on selling your home and moving to Florida? Or will you buy an RV and see America? Perhaps you are thinking about moving in with your children; after all, they probably lived with you for more years than you ever thought they would…and now is the time to plan your revenge!

Seriously, though, a very important decision that you need to make on your journey towards retirement is where you plan to live. For purposes of this book, let us assume that you want to remain in your present home, but at the same time you want to make sure you are secure enough (both financially and otherwise) to enjoy your golden years.

A new report by the American Association of Retired Persons shows that 70 percent of Americans already have made at least one change to their home to make it easier to get around. This is mainly because 80 percent of seniors prefer to live at home in their later years rather move to a retirement community.

As you grow older, you will realize that your present home may need some additional improvements to handle the "age factor." These may include:

- extra lighting

- grab bars and other bathroom safety features

- handrails on both sides of stairs

- non-skid rugs

That's just the tip of the iceberg when it comes to "age factor" improvements you will need to make if you decide to remain in your own home after you retire.

Of course, there are other options to consider, including assisted living communities, 55-plus communities, etc. Let's take a quick look at the pros and cons of those two options.

Assisted Living Communities – Pros

- help with activities of daily living, such as bathing, dressing, eating, mobility and using the bathroom

- meals at predictable times in a common area

- transportation to appointments, shopping, entertainment, etc. (some assisted living facilities have on-site medical care options)

- management of medications

- housekeeping and laundry services

- health, exercise, and wellness programs and equipment

- socialization through living near others and through scheduled programs

- secure environment

Assisted Living Communities – Cons

- possible navigation difficulties

- limited hours for visitors and entertaining

- getting rid of most of your possessions

- fears of losing touch with family and friends

- loss of personal autonomy – too many bosses

55-plus community – Pros

- brand-new home, at least for you

- no yard maintenance

- few restrictions on visitors and entertainment (but check your deed)

- possible "furnished option"

- lots of activities: classes, dancing, parties and other opportunities to socialize with your new neighbors

55-plus community – Cons

- leaving your own home

- only other seniors for neighbors

- no opportunity to care for own lawn and outdoor area

- restrictions on number of vehicles

In the end, it's a personal decision as to where you live. If you still have a little time before having to take a serious look at your future housing options, make sure you do your research carefully and talk with other people who have already taken the plunge.

What is "Aging in Place"?

"Aging in place is the ability to live in one's own home and community safely, independently and comfortably, regardless of age, income or ability level." - **Centers for Disease Control and Prevention.**

As we grow older, our needs change as our bodies and abilities change. Let's face it, a consequence of growing old is physical weakness–our ability lessens to do the activities which we could easily do when we were younger. Old age also increases the risk of health problems and accidents; and such factors may force us to leave our homes and enter a senior living facility. Given the choice, would you choose to leave your home for years? The answer for most seniors is a resounding "No!"

Aging in place, also known as "aging at home," means living at home (wherever that may be) as one ages. A senior is allowed to live in his own home as long as he is able without being forced to move to a nursing home, retirement center or other institutional or health care facility. Aging in place also means community involvement and policy changes for housing, transportation and land use to accommodate this movement to maintain and ensure the quality of senior life.

Benefits of Aging in Place

Six reasons aging in place could be the best option for you:

- **Stay exactly where you are.**

Many people dream about retiring to an exciting place= a chateau, a houseboat, or a motorhome where you can travel anywhere you want and satisfy the vagabond in you. Despite these fantasies, something inside you wants the comforts of an old and familiar place – your home, with its familiar and time-worn appeal that engenders feelings of comfort and trust.

This is the essence of aging in place; staying where your heart belongs. You won't need to make new friends. You won't need to pull up your roots. You won't need to worry about finding the nearest grocery store or remember new directions to the closest bus stop. You get to remain in a place where you have lived a good portion of your life.

- **Cut costs.**

Staying in place will help you cut costs. Inflation is an issue. There are taxes to pay and additional health expenses to worry about. Plus you might like to travel, at least to visit family. But every dime you spend on moving expenses is a dime out of your retirement funds.

- **Stay safe and comfortable.**

Your own belongings, familiar surroundings and people provide a feeling of comfort and safety.

- **Remain independent.**

Whether others admit it or not, living in a nursing home or other health care facility will restrict your independence in some ways. You may need to depend on others even if you feel you can do it. You will not be able to control your own life to the extent you have in the past.

- **Be happy.**

Take a look around, and you may see signs of incredible blessings right where you are. Being able to live with or near your family, see them grow, watch them learn to stand on their own gives you happiness.

Risks of Aging in Place

Aging in place can be very beneficial, but there are risks associated with it too. These risks include:

Living in unsafe places

One risk is living in a place unconducive to your overall well-being and health. Some seniors have no choice but to age in place since they do not have the necessary resources to move to other facilities. This could put them at risk of living in a place that is not conducive to comfort, security, safety and health. Such a risk worsens in neighborhoods with high crime, violence, loitering and poor access to good food. Unsafe neighborhoods can worsen physical decline also among older adults as they may leave their homes less and access local services less.

Increased risk with health issues

You may experience age-related changes which include heart disease, Alzheimer's, diabetes, hearing loss, vision problems and others. These health conditions may pose problems for you if you are intent on living alone. For instance, you may not be able to call for help when emergency situations occur.

Of course, living with your family can also be problematic, particularly if no family members are knowledgeable about such conditions.

Some people may even opt not to disclose their current health conditions as they are afraid of putting stress on their loved ones.

Increased risk for injuries

Physical problems, home and community hazards, solitary living conditions, functional impairment, decreased social support and poor nutrition place you at a higher risk for injuries, which might include bumps and bruises, car accidents and falls. The leading cause of injury leading to a hospital stay is falls, which may further lead to brain injuries and even death.

Minimizing Risk with Aging in Place

In a joint research report conducted by the National Conference of State Legislatures and the American Association of Retired Persons (AARP), important factors for successfully implementing an aging-in- place plan include:

Housing

The primary factor that should be considered in aging in place is housing. This requires that older individuals have a living space as ideal for them as possible. Preferably, the community should have an array of housing alternatives that are both affordable and accessible to older adults with varying assets and incomes. Below are possible dangers in the home.

Lighting

Poorly lit homes create fall, fire and cooking hazards, and can even make older adults easier targets for criminals. Additionally, seniors may develop eye problems; hence, it is critical that rooms, halls, stairs and walkways are well lit. You may also want to consider installing motion sensors in bathrooms and entryways.

Clutter

Piles of materials near doors and on counters and stairs can cause injuries and falls.

Temperature

A caregiver should be aware of home temperature. Older adults may not realize that their space is overheated or frigidly cold. Or if they do realize, they may be trying to save on heating or air conditioning costs. Either way, it is important to check on them regularly in order to avoid hypothermia or heat exhaustion.

Bathroom hazards

The bathroom of an older adult poses numerous safety hazards. Non-skid mats and grab bars should be installed in the bathroom to avoid falls and other accidents. The water heater should always be turned down on a safe level to avoid thermal burn, especially with seniors diagnosed with diabetes and experiencing diminished feeling of their extremities.

Communication

For emergencies, it is critical that older adults are capable of communicating with others and possess the knowledge to operate any equipment necessary for that communication (e.g., cordless phone, cell phone). Caregivers may also opt to use monitoring systems to check on seniors.

Transportation

Traveling safely within one's community or beyond is important for older adults to be able to engage socially, not to mention helping seniors maintain a positive and healthy outlook. Older non-driving adults rely heavily on public transportation. It is important to ensure quality transportation for all age groups, but particularly for seniors.

What Are the Costs of Long Term Care?

In the early years of retirement we are able to enjoy our rewards, but eventually the years begin to catch up with us. For so long it fell to us to take care of others, but as time marches on we find it harder and harder even to take care of ourselves.

We may have passed our prime, but we still have many years to enjoy life and the company of those we love. No one wants to become a burden, but there will come a time when we will need some assistance to get through the daily business of living. When that time comes, we will need to understand long term care services.

What Are Long Term Care Services?

Long-term care for seniors incorporates personal care services required by people who can no longer provide for themselves. In past generations, family members provided this sort of care. But today, between the busy modern lifestyle and the senior's desire not to become a burden, long-term care is often outsourced, at least partially.

The polar opposite of the active retirement of our dreams is to wind up forgotten in an "old folks' home." There will always be a need for nursing homes, but many seniors are happier and better served aging in place.

Long-term care services cover a spectrum which ideally includes most seniors' needs. How much long-term care each senior needs depends largely on how much assistance he needs with "activities of daily living."

Homemaker Services

The most basic level of elder-care is family and friends occasionally checking in on the seniors in their lives. This is often referred to as informal care; informal because no one is paid for the service. Moving up the ladder of formal senior care, we then encounter homemaker services. State, community or religious organizations often provide such homemaker services. Services vary but usually include assistance with light housework, cooking and companionship. Some will provide more personal services such as assistance with dressing and bathing. Homemaker services can delay or prevent institutionalized care.

According to Families USA, the average cost of homemaker services is around $19 per hour. Actual cost depends on a number of factors, including the geographic area and whether the service is provided by a commercial or civic organization.

Home Health Aides

Homemaker services and home health aides both contribute to senior quality of life by assisting with activities of daily living. In addition to companionship, light housekeeping and personal assistance, the home health aide is also a trained medical professional.

The senior's physician often prescribes home health aide services and the required level of care. The aide may work for a public agency or be hired directly by the senior's family.

Local governmental authority licenses and certifies health aides, but most aides will at least receive on-the-job training from a nurse or other health professional. Home health aides who work for an agency funded by Medicare or Medicaid must have at least 75 hours of medical training and at least 16 hours of supervised practical experience, in addition to passing a competency examination or state certification.

As a healthcare professional, the home aide will monitor the senior's condition and may be involved in some therapeutic protocols under the doctor's supervision.

Families USA says that the average cost for home health aides is $21 per hour. If the senior requires three hours of assistance daily, five days a week, this can cost upwards of $16,000 annually.

Adult Day Care

The assumption with homemaker services and part-time health aide services is that the senior is independent enough to take care of herself when the companion is not around. However, there may come a time when a senior needs almost full-time supervision and aid.

A full-time home health aide is one solution, but most often a family member takes on the duties of caregiver. Since it is unreasonable to expect the caregiver to be "on" 24/7, some sort of respite care is needed to allow the caregiver to work outside the home or just to enjoy a well-earned break.

Adult day care is an increasingly popular option for respite care. Most adult day care centers provide daytime services five days a week. The centers tend to focus on medical care and supervision, Alzheimer's care, and social interaction and activities. Adult day care centers are usually affiliated with senior service providers, health care centers or elder-care agencies.

The average cost of adult day care is $67 a day, according to Families USA, but prices vary by type of provider and level of care. For instance, supervision of an Alzheimer patient requires a good deal more staff interaction and attention than a social interaction group at the local community center.

Assisted Living Facilities

If a senior requires more assistance with activities of daily living than can be provided in the home, an assisted living facility can provide the necessary support.

There is an understandable stigma against "placing mama in a home," but living conditions and level of care in an assisted living facility are often better than a senior would have living on his own. In addition, many mentally competent seniors gladly make their own decision to transition to assisted living. Assisted living can range from small board-and-care homes with one or two seniors living in a spare bedroom, to professionally run small group homes, to large corporate facilities with hundreds of residents.

The assisted living center cannot provide the level of care a nursing home could, but most will have a medical staff and will work with the senior's primary health care provider. A larger facility may resemble an apartment complex. Residents will have their own apartments and staff will provide light housekeeping and laundry services, along with assistance with activities of daily living.

Assisted living facility residents generally have more freedom and independence than they would in a nursing home. The level of care is not as great, but neither is the costs.

The Assisted Living Federation of America states that the average cost of a one-bedroom apartment in an assisted living residence is $3,022 per month. The Federation further states that assisted living is usually less expensive than home care or nursing homes in the same geographic area.

Nursing Homes

For many people, the terms "nursing home" and "old folk's home" are interchangeable. The level of care given at a skilled nursing facility is one step below what would be given at a hospital, and frankly, often a good deal more than most seniors will require.

Nursing homes are usually set up like a hospital, with a central nurse's station on each floor and licensed nurses on the premises at all times. There is a recent trend to give nursing homes a more home-like look and feel. A newer facility may have comfortable common areas to facilitate socialization between residents and to encourage family visitation. Although they are primarily designed to ease patient care, some facilities are even set up so that couples can remain together.

AARP warns that the average cost of nursing home care is $50,000 annually, and increasing. That rate has a great deal of variation by location, but nursing home care carries an enormous potential to eat up a family's savings. Failure to purchase long-term care insurance presents the biggest threat to seniors needing nursing home financing. Medicare may cover short-term nursing home stays. Medicaid can pick up nursing home costs but will only do so after the patient's savings are exhausted.

The Future of Long Term Care Costs

When we look at cost trends of long-term care, we see some rather simple economic concepts at work. Whether economic theories are correct or not, one thing is obvious: the cost of long-term care is increasing and will continue to do so.

The most important reason for this is the basic economic law of supply and demand: children of the Baby Boom are rapidly approaching the age when many of them will require long-term care. With greater demand on the long-term care system, prices will go up.

As the long-term care industry expands and affects more seniors, it also faces greater regulation. The intent of regulatory supervision of this particular industry is to increase the safety of our seniors. That greater regulation will mean greater costs is a given.

Some look to the insurance industry to come to the rescue. In the early years of this century, long-term care insurance was expected to be the industry's "next big thing." Then, there were more than 100 companies offering coverage, but today there are less than a dozen. Consumers simply did not buy long term care insurance, and when they did it was not profitable for the insurance carriers. The carriers responded by raising premiums and decreasing benefits, further lowering consumer enthusiasm for the coverage.

Many families have been forced to turn to their personal savings to deal with long-term care costs. However, it should be kept in mind that these savings took a beating during the recent recession. Savings are recovering as the economy moves forward, although perhaps not as fast as the rise in long-term care cost.

What is the Cost of Long Term Care in Your Area?

The insurance industry has a vested interest in keeping track of long-term care costs in different regions. Several companies are happy to share this information with consumers using an interactive map.

Genworth Financial has been conducting their annual Cost of Care Survey since 2004. The current survey (https://www.genworth. com/corporate/about-genworth/industry-expertise/cost-of-care. html) presents cost information from 437 regions across the United States. John Hancock presents similar information, but some users find their map (http://www.johnhancockltc.com/individual/map/ JHLTC_CostofCare_v5.html) to be more user friendly.

A2.

The Government Benefits Safety Net

Chapter 1 highlights many of the costs of retirement, while this chapter addresses the benefits that may be available to you through the government. Bear in mind that the government intends these programs and services as a safety net, not as your primary retirement funds.

Social Security

Most of us are concerned with just two aspects of the Social Security system: (1) benefits and (2) taxes which support them, usually not in that order!

We can all remember the excitement we felt as a kid with our first real job, reading the statement attached to our first paycheck and wondering, "Who the heck is this FICA person and why are they taking so much of my money?" The Federal Insurance Contribution Act tax is paid by every worker. The FICA tax is a proportion of each worker's gross wages, up to a maximum threshold of $113,700 (as of 2013). Current withholding is 6.2% for Social Security and 2.45% for Medicare, totaling 7.65% of each worker's pay. Employers are required to match that amount, and self-employed workers pay into the Self Employment Contributions Act tax (SECA) at the full 15.3% rate.

Since the benefits that retirees can expect to receive are based on their tax contribution, it is easy to think of Social Security as a savings plan for retirement. This is a mistake. The taxes collected each year go towards paying benefits. Most years, the economy is strong enough that more tax is collected than is needed to pay benefits. The extra money goes into a trust fund which invests the money in US Treasury bonds, considered the safest investment in the world. In years when there are not enough taxes collected to cover the benefits, the trust fund redeems the bonds (with interest) to cover the shortfall.

Since the US economy and employment have grown in most years after passage of the original Social Security Act in 1935, there has been little worry about the taxes and trust fund being able to cover the benefits. However, as the Baby Boomer generation move toward retirement age and beyond, there is a shrinking pool of young workers to pay FICA and SECA taxes, placing a strain on the trust fund. This is the basis for concerns that "Social Security is running out of money." Whether or not these are valid fears or simply political posturing is a discussion beyond the scope of this chapter.

When Do You First Get Social Security?

We usually consider Social Security in relation to retirement, but the system also benefits survivors of a deceased worker, leaving dependent spouses and/or children, as well as workers who are disabled and unable to work. Workers are eligible to retire with full Social Security benefits when they reach "full retirement age," which is 65-67. (Persons born after 1959 reach full retirement age at 67.) Workers may opt to retire early at 62 but will receive a lower benefit rate. Conversely, workers who delay retirement beyond 67 will receive a higher benefit.

Note: If you are full retirement age, you can apply for Social Security and then request to have payments suspended. That way, your spouse can receive a spouse's benefit, and you can continue to earn delayed benefits until age 70. Check with a counsellor, however, to see whether this tactic will adversely impact other benefits such as Medicare.

Social Security Eligibility:

Since the inception of the Social Security system, Social Security numbers have become the de facto identification method for US residents, with the number actually being required for several activities, from paying taxes to personal identification with banks, insurance companies and private businesses.

To qualify for Social Security retirement benefits, usually a person must have worked at least 10 years and earned at least $4250 per year.

How Much Will You Get?

Each retiree's benefit level is based on his average wage for the previous 35 years. Since the tax contribution is a fixed percentage of the wage, it would seem natural that the more you contribute, the greater benefit you would receive. However, the benefit is figured on a sliding scale so that those who earn less receive a higher proportion of their contribution. This is a reflection of the original intent of Social Security, which was to provide a hedge against poverty for seniors in modern times.

The IRS tracks each worker's wages and reports that amount to the Social Security Administration. The SSA provides on-line calculators on its website, allowing you to estimate your potential benefit level.

Generally, retirement benefits increase each December when the cost of living adjustment (COLA) goes into effect. The previous year's inflation rate determines this year's COLA, so there is no guarantee of a particular annual increase or of any increase at all.

Costs to You:

Since participation in Social Security is mandatory for nearly all wage and salary earners, the FICA or SECA tax is unavoidable. This causes some controversy since many investors would prefer to make their own investments with an eye toward making a greater return than under the current system. In all likelihood the return would be greater with private investment, but it would also leave the lowest wage earners, those who are going to need the support of Social Security the most, out in the cold.

Social Security was never meant to be the sole source of income for our senior citizens; however, after the recent pension fund crisis, Social Security benefits have grown in importance to seniors beyond the lower income brackets. The amount you receive when you first get benefits sets the base for the amount you will receive for the rest of your life.

If you are wondering what might be the best time to start collecting Social Security benefits, one important factor to take into account is how long you might live. According to current data compiled by the Social Security Administration:

- A man reaching age 65 today can expect to live, on average, until age 84.

- A woman turning age 65 today can expect to live, on average, until age 86.

Besides life expectancy, following are other questions you may want to consider:

- Are you still working?

- Do you come from a long-lived family?

- How is your health?

- Will you still have health insurance?

- Are you eligible for benefits on someone else's insurance?

- Do you have other income to support you if you decide to delay taking benefits?

What is Medicare?

Medicare is a federal health insurance program designed to provide certain health care needs of senior citizens age 65 and older. The program also covers some younger persons with certain specific conditions. Health care was not specifically a part of the 1935 Social Security Act; however, it quickly became apparent that seniors began to experience an increased need for medical servioces at a point in their lives when they were least able to pay for those services. Under the leadership of President

Johnson, Congress created Medicare in 1965 through Title XVIII of the Social Security Act.

Social Security Survivor Benefits

If you are working and paying into Social Security, some of the Social Security taxes you pay goes toward survivor's insurance. In fact, the value of the survivor's insurance you have under Social Security is probably more than the value of your current life insurance.

If you are married **and** both of you are wage earners, you should consider survivors benefits from both perspectives.

When you die, members of your family could be eligible for benefits based on your earnings. Social Security has created some great information called "Planning for Your Survivors," which explains how you earn benefits and who qualifies for them.

If your spouse or parent dies, you and your family could be eligible to receive benefits based on their earnings. To learn about the survivors' benefits that may be available to you, go to the "If You Are the Survivor" section on the Social Security Website.

Planning For Your Survivors

As you plan for the future, you'll want to think about what your family would need if you should die now. Social Security can help your family if you have earned enough Social Security credits through your work.

How You Earn Social Security Survivors Benefits

You can earn up to four credits each year. In 2013, for example, you earn one credit for each $1,160 of wages or self-employment income. When you have earned $4,640, you have earned your four credits for the year.

The number of credits needed to provide benefits for your survivors depends on your age when you die. The younger a person is, the fewer credits he or she must have for family members to receive survivors' benefits. But no one needs more than 40 credits (10 years of work) to be eligible for any Social Security benefit.

However, benefits can be paid to your children and your spouse who is caring for the children even if you don't have the required number of credits. They can get benefits if you have credit for one and one-half years of work (6 credits) in the three years just before your death.

Survivors Benefits for Your Widow Or Widower

You probably know people who are receiving Social Security survivors' benefits because they're a widow or widower. At present, there are about 5 million widows and widowers receiving monthly Social Security benefits based on their deceased spouse's earnings record. And, for many of those survivors, particularly aged women, those benefits are keeping them out of poverty.

- Your widow or widower can receive:

  ○ Reduced benefits as early as age 60 or full benefits at full retirement age or older.

  ○ Benefits as early as age 50 if he or she is disabled AND their disability started before or within seven years of your death.

Note: If a widow or widower who is caring for your children receives Social Security benefits, he or she is still eligible if their disability starts before those payments end or within seven years after they end.

A widow, widower or surviving divorced spouse cannot apply online for survivors' benefits. However, they can get the process started by completing an "Adult Disability Report" before they contact Social Security.

Note: Social Security uses the same "definition of disability" for widows and widowers as they do for workers.

If your widow or widower remarries after they reach age 60 (age 50 if disabled), the remarriage will not affect their eligibility for survivors benefits.

Your widow or widower who has not remarried can receive survivor's benefits at any age if she or he takes care of you.

When Can You Get Medicare?

Medicare covers most people aged 65 and older; younger disabled persons receiving Social Security Disability Insurance (SSDI); and persons with end-stage renal disease (ESRD) and amyotrophic lateral sclerosis (Lou Gehrig's Disease).

Eligibility:

Nearly all Americans and legal residents of the US qualify for Medicare when they reach 65. Medicare was one of President Johnson's "Great Society" programs, and it is credited as helping to end segregation of waiting rooms since doctors and hospitals who practiced racial discrimination would not qualify for payment under Medicare.

How Much Will You Get under Medicare?

Medicare is divided into different parts: Part A (Hospital Insurance), Part B (Supplemental Medical Insurance), Part C (Medicare Advantage Plans) and Part D (Prescription Drug Coverage).

Although Part A is called Hospital Coverage, it also covers some skilled nursing home care, some in-home care and some hospice care. Participation in Part B is voluntary and applies to doctor's services, outpatient hospital care, speech and physical therapy, ambulance services and some home health care and medical equipment. The government calls Parts A and B "Original Medicare".

Part D is voluntary and helps to cover the costs of prescription drugs. This coverage is not standardized and is administered by one of several private insurance companies, each of which offer their own plans and lists of drugs. Participation may require payment of a premium and deductible.

Medicare Part C (Medicare + 'Choice') allows participants to design coverage which suits their medical needs. Part C plans work with Health Maintenance Organizations (HMOs), Preferred Provider Organizations (PPOs), medical specialists and private insurers. Plans can be designed which take special needs into consideration such as diabetes.

Costs to You:

Contributions from FICA and SECA taxes fund Medicare. Congress never intended Medicare to fund full payment for all medical services; thus, many Medicare programs have a premium and co-pays, although some have no premium at all.

Most Part A participants do not pay a monthly premium for that part of the program since they contributed through their FICA taxes. Those who did not work the minimum amount of time to qualify for Part A can buy into the program for a monthly premium.

Part B participation requires a monthly premium ($104.90 in 2013/2014) which is normally deducted from the Social Security check. Those who qualify for Medicare but are not receiving a Social Security check may be billed quarterly.

There may or may not be a premium for Parts C and D, depending on the individual private plan the recipient chooses.

What is Medicaid?

It is easy to confuse Medicare and Medicaid. They were both created in 1965 under the Johnson administration, and they have similar names and functions. Medicare, as discussed above, was designed to provide health care assistance to the elderly, while Medicaid provides low cost or free health care to the poor.

The Medicaid program is a partnership between the federal government and each state. (States are not required to participate in Medicaid, but all fifty do.) The federal government funds up to half of each state's Medicaid program, with the more affluent states receiving less funding; each state is responsible for regulating and administering its program. For this reason, essentially 50 different Medicaid programs exist.

Medicaid funds hospitalization, nursing care, skilled nursing facility care and home care, among other services, to those who qualify. Although eligibility is mainly based on income and assets, these are not the only qualifying conditions.

When can you get Medicaid?

Since Medicaid is designed to provide health coverage to the poor, to qualify you must prove your eligibility rather than reaching a particular age as with Social Security or Medicare. Since most seniors are retired and unable to work, they often meet the low income requirement. Since Medicaid can provide valuable assistance in funding long-term residential care, a cottage industry within the legal profession has sprung up to assist seniors in divesting their assets so that they can qualify for Medicaid assistance.

Eligibility:

Each state sets its own eligibility requirements for Medicaid, but they must meet federal guidelines to receive matching federal funding. Beginning in 2014, states must allow persons with an income of 133% of the poverty line to qualify, including adults with no dependent children. Other qualifying categories include low-income children, pregnant women, parents of Medicaid eligible children, as well as low- income seniors. There is a recognized class of so-called "dual eligible" who qualify for both Medicare and Medicaid. These are often persons over the age of 65 living in nursing homes.

How Much Do You Get?

Medicaid is a primary funding source for skilled nursing facility care. Since Medicaid is administered differently by each state, actual benefits and coverage may differ, but nursing facility care is always required to be deemed medically necessary and take place in a facility which is licensed by the state. Medicaid coverage for nursing facility services will only be provided when all other private coverage, resources and assets are exhausted.

Costs to You:

Medicaid costs to those receiving services depend upon the individual state and program. Some programs may charge a small fee or co-pay for services, although certain vulnerable groups, including children and pregnant women, are specifically exempt from these out-of-pocket costs or co-pay requirements.

A3.

Strategies to Pay for Retirement

Many people try not to worry about retirement. After all, no one wants to think about how much money it will take just to continue the current standard of living, especially when the economy has not been very cooperative over the past decade or so.

Experts advise us to start saving for retirement the moment they begin working. Hats off to anyone who has been able to launch a retirement savings plan while in their twenties - when they reach their sixties, well, let's just say they won't have to worry about missing the senior dinner special at the local eatery! But for some of us, that plan to start saving early and keep at it until retirement turns out to be unworkable.

By some counts, fewer than half of Americans have ever tried to calculate how much they'll need for retirement. And those who do? In one recent survey, half told pollsters they just guessed.

A new poll for NPR, the Robert Wood Johnson Foundation and Harvard School of Public Health finds retirement is proving more difficult than expected for many Americans, in large part because they haven't saved enough.

Now Is the Time to Economize

If you are really serious about wanting to save more money for your retirement years, then now is the time to economize. No doubt there are areas in your life where you can tighten your belt and trim expenses. While it will not be easy or pleasant at first, if you create a plan that works for you and your family, and if you enlist their aid, it *will* work.

Here are some tips that will help you cut back on expenses:

- Categorize your expenses as *wants* and *needs*. *Needs* include housing, basic utilities, childcare, etc. *Wants* could include going out to eat, high fashion (or even more clothes than you actually *need*), newest electronics, etc. *Wants* we can space out over time. Do not let your impulses determine major purchases. Postpone unplanned purchases 24 hours so you can rethink your plan.

- Avoid shopping when you are down, depressed, tired or hungry. If you have children, shop without them to reduce any sense of being rushed; feeling rushed may lead to impulse purchases. In addition, if my visits to the grocery store lately are any indication, children inevitably try to wheedle their parents into buying them *something*. It is a great idea to ease them out of that impulse to demand a toy or a treat by simply leaving them at home!

- Before purchasing an item, ask yourself, "Why?" Perhaps you are purchasing some things just because it feels good to buy and to spend money.

- Reduce the number of trips you make to the store. Wait until there are things you need. Plan purchases around seasonal sales throughout the year.

- Pre-shop to stop spending leaks. Decide what you want and why you want it before you go shopping. Make it a habit to compare prices and values. If at all possible, try out or try on the item before you buy it. This practice will provide you with the opportunity to determine if the item will meet your needs.

- Compare the cost per unit of items available in different sizes. It is not always cheaper to buy in bulk. Save on food by planning meals with abundant seasonal items and supermarket specials. Take a carefully prepared list to the grocery store and stick to it. Use point-of-sale information for comparing product quality and price.

- Save on clothes by planning your wardrobe. Never buy clothes when they first hit the stores; wait for sales. Check for fit, and buy only clothes that fit comfortably. Coordinate your clothing and accessory items. Examine care labels for fiber content and cleaning instructions. By taking proper care of your clothes, you will make them last longer and save money on replacements.

- Save on transportation by selecting an automobile that adequately meets your needs, but does so without extremely high cost. A fuel-efficient automobile will yield substantial savings over time. Planning trips in logical sequences instead of doubling back to places you have already been also saves fuel.

- If you have debts, accelerate repayment. There is little reason to retain savings that earns 3% interest while you still owe installment debts and loans that carry true interest rates of 12–22%.

- For your banking services, select an institution with the lowest service charges on your accounts. Some banks do not charge anything as long as you keep your checking account above a certain minimum amount.

- Buy property insurance at a reasonable cost. In general, you save by combining several types of coverage in one policy.

A homeowner's package policy costs less than separate fire, theft, and liability insurance policies. Many insurance companies offer discounts if you place both your homeowner's and auto insurance with them.

- When buying insurance, avoid buying on a weekly or installment basis. This costs you much more than payments made every six months or annually.

- House repairs can be costly. Get competitive bids from reputable firms before the work is started. Maintain your furnace or air-conditioner by remembering to change or clean the air return filter regularly. Not only is it less efficient to have the fan pull air through a dirty filter, but also a clogged filter can burn out the motor and cost you a repair bill.

- Take steps to conserve heat, cool air and hot water. Use weather stripping, caulking and insulation to reduce utility bills. Water leaks are not only annoying but also expensive. A series of seemingly minor leaks can run your water usage up several thousand gallons a year. Water your lawn, not the pavement. A carelessly placed or over powerful sprinkler can send many dollars' worth of water washing down the sidewalk and into the gutter each year. Consider soaker hoses.

When buying a household appliance, remember that the bottom-of-the-line model will perform its intended function without the frills of the more expensive top-of-the-line model.

Compare the included warranty coverage of the appliances you are considering in your purchase decision since many extended warranties and service contracts are overpriced and never needed during their lifetime. The very best way to save on the high cost of repairs is to avoid them.

Move to a Less Expensive Area

The cost of living is creeping ever upward. It seems as if everything is going up in price. Cutting back on your daily living expenses is one way to save money for retirement, and another way is to move to a less expensive part of the country. While that might not be an option for many people who desire to continue living close to children and grandchildren, others may serious consider a move.

Get a Job

Another way to supplement your income and increase your savings is to take a second job. Or, if you are already retired, start a new job. (Note: if you are collecting Social Security, make sure you know how much you will be able to earn by working so that you do not interfere with your monthly benefits.)

According to the website Suite 101, advice abounds on good occupations for seniors. It is amazing to see how many people advise seniors to become a Wal-Mart greeter. (Update: In some geographic areas at least, Walmart no longer hires greeters.) While this job may have its benefits and may be a good fit for some people, new retirees should be aware that there are other options out there:

- Many retired professionals become consultants. One segment in need of experienced, professional advice is new or growing small businesses.

- Seniors can become independent contractors or freelancers.

- A retiree can start a small business based on a hobby or area of expertise.

In short, there are many activities suitable for retired people. With the right mindset, seniors can turn their golden years into a productive and fulfilling period in their lives.

Save Money with Senior Discounts

By now you have probably seen a few senior citizens wearing a baseball cap with the words "I'm a senior, where's my discount?" And while you might have thought it was cute at the time, don't underestimate the "buying and saving" power of a senior discount!

Here's some info to help you get in the right frame of mind about seniors and saving money – you'll find discounts for the following:

Food and Entertainment

Denny's, Starbucks, Outback Steakhouse, Texas Roadhouse, Regal Cinema, Olive Garden, and Redo Lobster.

Shopping

1-800-Flowers, Tangier Outlets, Sears, J.C. Penney's, Macy's, Nordstrom's, Hallmark, Target and Walmart.

Hotels & Resorts

MGM Grand, Best Western, Holiday Inn, Sleep Inn, Days Inn, Double Tree, Sheraton, Econo Lodge, and Hilton.

Thanks to the Internet, finding your next senior discount is only a click away. But it's up to YOU to make sure you take advantage of all of the savings that are out there!

Paying For Long-Term Care

Life Insurance

Some companies offer an accelerated benefits rider that you can add to your life insurance policy for an additional premium. This rider allows you to access your death benefit early if you are diagnosed with a long-term, catastrophic, or terminal illness. The amount you withdraw to pay for long-term care will be subtracted from the death benefit that will go to your beneficiaries when you die.

There are also some life insurance policies that offer long-term care insurance as a rider. If your policy includes any of these options, you may be able to pay for long-term care with the proceeds.

Annuity Contracts

Some annuity contracts allow you to withdraw money without a penalty to pay for long-term care services. If your contract includes this option, you may be able to pay for long-term care expenses with your annuity.

Viatical and Life Settlements

Some companies purchase life insurance policies and pay a percentage of the policy's death benefit in return. If you are terminally ill and have a life expectancy of two years or less, this settlement is called a viatical settlement. If you no longer want or need your policy, it's called a life settlement.

If you sell your policy, the buyer becomes the policy owner, pays the premiums, and collects the policy's benefit when you die. Make sure you check with your insurance company about any cash value you may have in your policy to determine if the cash value is more beneficial to you than selling the policy.

Reverse Mortgages

If you own a home, you may be able to get a reverse mortgage. Reverse mortgages are special home loans available to people 62 and over. They allow you to convert part of the equity you've built up in your home into income without having to sell the home or take out a second mortgage. No payments are due on the loan until the home is no longer your primary residence. People use income from a reverse mortgage for many purposes including paying living expenses, paying medical bills, for long-term care expenses, or even for vacations. This book contains in-depth discussions of reverse mortgages and their uses.

A4.

Saving for Retirement

Some people come from wealthy families and rightly expect a hefty inheritance, in which case they don't need Social Security anyway. But that would not be you or me, or we would probably not be reading this book! So how to put together the money you'll need to retire? And how do you know how much you'll need?

Since there are so many variables in trying to answer this last question, the best answer can only be a rough estimate For instance, consider the all-important issue of life expectancy. The Social Security Administration offers a life expectancy calculator at http://www.ssa.gov/planners/lifeexpectancy.htm - giving average life expectancy for male and female.

However, even the SSA calls its calculator "simple," and says that what you'll get if you use it is only a "rough" estimate. This is because the calculator ignores a wide array of factors that definitely influence the life expectancy of a particular individual: (1) your family history, (2) your own history and lifestyle, (3) and your current health.

Just consider a few of the possibilities (good and bad) lurking in these three seemingly simple concepts: For instance, do you or your family members have a history of cancer or heart disease or genetically transmitted disease? Has excessive alcohol use or other substance abuse been a factor? Have you had any serious accidents? Have you had any serious illnesses which have left you with lingering health problems or which are likely to recur? Are you prone to serious depression? Do you have healthy relationships with family and friends? Do you exercise regularly? Do you smoke or do you live with a smoker? Do you exercise your mind by reading and learning new things? Do you have hobbies that you enjoy; or do you just sit and watch TV all day?

The list of questions is endless, and, of course, even if you could identify all of the proper questions and answer them, you would still not be sure how much weight to give to each factor. The point, though, is that the SSA life expectancy calculator can only tell you the *average* age an American man or woman will live. *How long you yourself will live is unknown*, which is why it is so hard to estimate how much money is enough money for retirement.

Face it. What we should do is take 10-20% of every *paycheck from the day we report to our very first job* and sock it away. But how many people do you know that have done that? Cindy Hounsell,

President of Women's Institute for a Secure Retirement, suggests one excellent source of retirement income is a 401(k), particularly if you've been paying into it from Day 1 of your work experience. (I know one fellow – changes my oil at Jiffy Lube, where he's worked all his adult life. Not a high-paying job, for sure, but according to him he's managed to set aside over $400,000.)

And some of the biggest mistakes you can make?

- Withdrawing *any* money from a 401(k) when you change jobs.

- Collecting Social Security too early.

- Saving at least a portion of any windfall money that comes your way.

- Cultivating thrifty habits, starting early. Try a meatless meal once a week. See how many times you've eaten out in the last month, and cut that down by 20%. Never buy retail. Give yourself a cooling off period when you're about to buy something, time to think whether you really need that item. NOW: For each of these thrifty suggestions, once a week calculate about how much money you saved by doing things the new way, and *save that amount. On a regular basis.*

Glossary – Reverse Mortgage and Associated Terms

A

AARP - American Association of Retired Persons.

Adjustment date - the date the interest rate changes on an adjustable-rate mortgage (ARM).

Acceleration clause – a contract provision setting out when a loan may be declared due and payable.

Adjustment period - the period between adjustment dates for an adjustable-rate mortgage (ARM).

Adjustable rate - an interest rate that changes, generally based on changes in a published market-rate index. *The LIBOR market-rate index is an example of such a market-rate index.*

Amortization - gradual repayment of a mortgage loan, both principal and interest, by installments; not used with reverse mortgages.

Annual percentage rate (APR) - the cost of credit, expressed as a yearly rate, including interest and mortgage insurance and loan origination fees. This allows the buyer to compare loans; however APR should not be confused with the actual note rate. *The APR on a reverse mortgage can be difficult to understand. Consult your reverse mortgage professional.*

Annuity - a monthly cash payment from an insurance company for the rest of your life. *You can get a monthly check for life or a defined length of time from a reverse mortgage as well.*

Appraisal - an estimate of how much a house or home would sell for if it sold on that date: also called "market value."

Appreciation - an increase in a house or home's value.

Assignment - transfer of a mortgage from one company to another.

Assumability - reverse mortgages are not assumable. *They can be refinanced, however.*

B

Broker - an individual or company that brings borrowers and lenders together for the purpose of loan origination. *Brokers often can provide the lowest cost loans because they can choose from the best of several different bank loan programs.*

C

Cap - a limit on the amount an adjustable interest rate may go up or down during a specified time period.

Certificate of counseling - a document issued by an FHA-approved counseling service company after a borrower has completed reverse mortgage counseling.

Closing - a meeting where documents are signed to "close the deal" on a mortgage loan; the time when a mortgage begins.

Closing costs - normally include origination fee, mortgage insurance, property taxes, charges for title insurance, recording fees and appraisal fees.

CMT rate – the constant maturity treasury rate, used as an interest rate index in the HECM program.

Condemnation – the court's official finding that a property is unfit for use: also, government taking of private property for public use by process of eminent domain.

Consumer reporting agency (Credit Bureau) - an organization that handles preparation of reports used by lenders to determine a potential borrower's credit history and other information from public records.

Counseling – Required before you get a person receives a reverse mortgage or HECM loan.

Counseling agency - An agency approved to perform required reverse mortgage counseling.

Credit line - a credit account that lets a borrower decide when to take money out and how much to take out; also known as a "line of credit."

Credit report - a report that details an individual's credit history, prepared by a credit bureau and used by a lender to determine if any federal liens exist against a reverse mortgage borrower.

Current interest rate - in the HECM program, the interest rate currently charged on a loan; it equals the one-year rate for US Treasury securities, plus a margin (see below).

D

Deferred payment loans (DPLs) - reverse mortgages that give a lump sum of cash to the borrower to repair or improve a home; usually offered by state or local governments.

Depreciation - a decrease in the value of a house or home.

E

Expected interest rate - in the HECM program, the interest rate used to determine a borrower's loan advance amounts, equaling the 10-year rate for US Treasury securities plus a margin.

F

Fannie Mae - private company that buys and sells mortgages; a government-sponsored business watched over by the federal government.

Federal Housing Administration (FHA) - the part of the US Department of Housing and Urban Development (HUD) that insures HECM loans.

Federally insured reverse mortgage - a reverse mortgage guaranteed by the federal government so you will always get what the loan promises; also, a home equity conversion mortgage (HECM).

Federal liens – Debts owed to a federal agency or loans taken out through a federal agency which must be paid before a reverse mortgage is closed or paid from the reverse mortgage proceeds.

First mortgage - the primary lien against a property.

Fixed monthly loan advances - payments of the same amount made to a reverse mortgage borrower each month.

G

Government backed - Most reverse mortgages are government backed.

Government insured - Most reverse mortgages are government insured.

Government regulated - Most reverse mortgages must comply with government regulations.

H

Homekeeper - Fannie Mae's reverse mortgage product that allows a borrower to use a reverse mortgage to purchase a home.

Home equity - the value of a home minus any money owed on it.

Home equity conversion - turning home equity into cash without having to lease your home or make regular loan repayments.

Home Equity Conversion Mortgage (HECM) - the only reverse mortgage program insured by the Federal Housing Administration, a federal government agency.

HELOC - Home equity line of credit

HUD-1 Statement - a document that provides an itemized list of funds payable at loan closing.

I

Index - the measure of interest rate changes a lender uses to decide the amount an interest rate on an ARM will change over time; Reverse mortgage rates are tied to US Treasury rates.

Initial interest rate - in the HECM program, the interest rate first charged on the loan beginning at closing; it equals the one-year rate for US Treasury securities, plus a margin.

Interest rate ceiling - for an adjustable-rate mortgage (ARM), the maximum interest rate as specified in the mortgage note.

Interest rate floor - for an adjustable-rate mortgage (ARM), the minimum interest rate as specified in the mortgage note.

J

Jumbo reverse mortgage - a reverse mortgage outside of government program guidelines that considers property values above $625,500.

L

Leftover equity - the sale price of the home minus the total amount owed on it and the cost of selling it; the amount the homeowner or heirs receive when the house is sold.

LIBOR - London inter-bank offer rate, a market-rate often used to set adjustable rate reverse mortgages.

Loan advances - payments made to a borrower, or to another party on behalf of a borrower.

Loan balance - the amount owed, including principal and interest; capped in a reverse mortgage by the value of the home when the loan is repaid.

Lump sum - a single loan advance at closing.

M

Margin - in the HECM program, the amount added to the one-year Treasury rate to determine the initial and current interest rates, and to the 10-year Treasury rate to determine the expected interest rate.

Maturity - when a loan must be repaid; that is, when it becomes "due and payable."

Mortgage - a legal document that pledges a property to a lender as security for repayment of a debt.

Mortgage banker - a company that originates mortgages exclusively for resale in the secondary mortgage market.

Mortgage broker - an individual or company that brings borrowers and lenders together for the purpose of loan origination.

Mortgagee - the party to a mortgage who makes the loan.

Mortgagor - the borrower in a mortgage agreement.

N

Non-recourse mortgage - a home loan in which the borrower can never owe more than the home's value at the time the loan is repaid.

Note - a legal document that obligates a borrower to repay a mortgage loan.

O

Origination - the process of setting up a mortgage, including preparation of documents.

Origination fee - a fee paid to the lender for originating and processing a loan application. The origination fee is stated in the form of points; two points equals two percent of appraised value, maximum claim amount or adjusted loan amount for reverse mortgages.

P

Pre-approval - the process of determining how much money you are eligible to borrow before you apply for a loan.

Property tax deferral (PTD) - reverse mortgages that pay annual property taxes; usually offered by state of local governments.

Proprietary reverse mortgage - a reverse mortgage product owned by a private company.

R

Real Estate Settlement Procedures Act (RESPA) - a consumer protection law that requires lenders to give borrowers advance notice of closing costs.

Recording - noting in the county registrar's office of the details of a properly executed legal document, such as a deed, a mortgage note or a satisfaction of mortgage, thereby making it a part of the public record.

Refinance - paying off one loan with the proceeds from a new loan, using the same property as security. Reverse annuity mortgage - a reverse mortgage in which a lump sum is used to purchase an annuity that gives the borrower a monthly income for life.

Reverse mortgage - a home loan that gives cash advances to a homeowner, requiring no repayment until a future time and capped by the value of the home when the loan is repaid.

Right of rescission - a borrower's right to cancel a home loan within three business days of closing.

S

Set aside - amounts taken from loan amount and set aside for future costs of servicing, taxes or insurances.

Start rate - one year US Treasury security weekly index plus mortgage rate margin (determined by lender/Fannie Mae).

Secondary mortgage market - where existing mortgages are bought and sold.

Servicing - administering a loan after closing, such as maintaining loan records and sending statements.

Shared equity - shared equity programs are no longer available (Aug 03).

Supplemental Security Income (SSI) - a federal monthly income program for low-income persons who are aged 65+, blind or disabled.

T

Tenure advances - fixed monthly loan advances for as long as a borrower lives in a home.

Term advances - fixed monthly loan advances for a specific period of time.

Total annual loan cost (TALC) rate - the projected annual average cost of a reverse mortgage, including all itemized costs.

T-rate - the rate for US Treasury securities; used to determine the initial, expected, and current interest rates for the HECM program.

Truth-in-Lending - a federal law that requires lenders to fully disclose, in writing, the terms and conditions of a mortgage, including the annual percentage rate (APR) and other charges.

U

Underwriting - the process of evaluating a loan application to determine the quality of the property and the amount a borrower may borrow.

Uninsured reverse mortgage - a reverse mortgage that becomes due and payable on a specific date.

Made in the USA
San Bernardino, CA
01 November 2014